FREE DVD  FREE DVD

Essential Test Tips DVD from Trivium Test Prep

Dear Customer,

Thank you for purchasing from Trivium Test Prep! Whether you're looking to join the military, get into college, or advance your career, we're honored to be a part of your journey.

To show our appreciation (and to help you relieve a little of that test-prep stress), we're offering a **FREE *CLEP College Algebra Essential Test Tips DVD**** by Trivium Test Prep. Our DVD includes 35 test preparation strategies that will help keep you calm and collected before and during your big exam. All we ask is that you email us your feedback and describe your experience with our product. Amazing, awful, or just so-so: we want to hear what you have to say!

To receive your **FREE *CLEP College Algebra Essential Test Tips DVD*,** please email us at 5star@ triviumtestprep.com. Include "Free 5 Star" in the subject line and the following information in your email:

1. The title of the product you purchased.
2. Your rating from 1 – 5 (with 5 being the best).
3. Your feedback about the product, including how our materials helped you meet your goals and ways in which we can improve our products.
4. Your full name and shipping address so we can send your **FREE *CLEP College Algebra Essential Test Tips DVD*.**

If you have any questions or concerns please feel free to contact us directly at 5star@triviumtestprep.com.

Thank you, and good luck with your studies!

* Please note that the free DVD is not included with this book. To receive the free DVD, please follow the instructions above.

CLEP College Algebra Study Guide 2017

CLEP Test Prep and Practice Tests for the CLEP College Algebra Examination

TABLE OF CONTENTS

INTRODUCTION i

1 NUMBER SYSTEMS AND OPERATIONS 1

Types of Numbers 1

Order of Operations 7

Fractions................................... 9

Ratios 11

Proportions............................... 12

Exponents and Radicals 13

Sequences and Series 16

2 ALGEBRAIC OPERATIONS 21

Algebraic Expressions 21

Operations with Expressions........ 22

3 EQUATIONS AND INEQUALITIES 27

Linear Equations 27

Linear Inequalities..................... 36

Quadratic Equations and Inequalities 42

Absolute Value Equations and Inequalities 50

4 FUNCTIONS 53

Working with Functions 53

Inverse Functions 57

Compound Functions............................ 59

Transforming Functions 60

Exponential and Logarithmic Functions. 62

Polynomial Functions............................ 69

Rational Functions 70

Radical Functions.................................. 74

Modeling Relationships.......................... 76

5 PRACTICE TEST 79

Answer Key 87

INTRODUCTION

Congratulations on choosing to take the CLEP College Algebra exam! By purchasing this book, you've taken an important step on your path to college.

This guide will provide you with a detailed overview of the CLEP College Algebra exam, so that you know exactly what to expect on test day. We'll take you through all the concepts covered on the exam and give you the opportunity to test your knowledge with practice questions. Even if it's been a while since you last took a major test, don't worry; we'll make sure you're more than ready!

What is the CLEP?

The College-Level Examination Program, or CLEP, offers standardized tests in thirty-three subjects. The CLEP assesses college-level knowledge and allows students to demonstrate that they have proficiency in a subject so that they may bypass the coursework. If a student passes the exam, he or she earns college credit without having to take a single class. Anyone can take the CLEP, but it is designed specifically for people who have had experiences that have allowed them to obtain substantial expertise outside of the classroom. This includes students who have been homeschooled or undertaken extensive independent study, students who studied outside of the United States, adults returning to school after being the workforce, and members of the military.

Approximately 2,900 colleges and universities in the United States grant CLEP credit. Each college or university determines which exams to accept and sets its own passing score for each exam. Typically, these range from fifty to sixty out of eighty points. Each college also decides how much credit an exam is worth. Colleges will usually offer three credits for an exam, but some schools offer more (depending on the test), and some may offer only an exemption from the requirement but no credit toward graduation. If credits are given, they are added to your transcript just like credits from your coursework would be. CLEP credits carry the same weight as any other earned credits.

What's on the CLEP College Algebra Exam?

The CLEP College Algebra exam gauges college-level content knowledge that would be found in a single-semester college algebra course. Test questions can be divided into two types: half of the questions will ask you to solve routine algebraic problems, while the other half will ask you to demonstrate your mastery of algebraic concepts by solving non-routine problems. Candidates are expected to demonstrate thorough conceptual knowledge of a range of topics including algebraic operations; linear and quadratic equations; inequalities and graphs; and algebraic, exponential, and logarithmic functions.

You will have ninety minutes to answer sixty multiple-choice questions, including unscored pre-test questions.

What's on the CLEP College Algebra Exam?

Content Area	Topics	Percentage of Exam
Algebraic Operations	Operations with exponents Factoring and expanding polynomials Operations with algebraic expressions Absolute value Properties of logarithms	25%
Equations and Inequalities	Linear equations and inequalities Quadratic equations and inequalities Absolute value equations and inequalities Systems of equations and inequalities Exponential and logarithmic equations	25%
Functions and their Properties	Definition and interpretation Representation/modeling Domain and range Algebra of functions Graphs and their properties Inverse functions	30%
Number Systems and Operations	Real numbers Complex numbers Sequences and series Factorials and the binomial theorem	20%

Test-takers are expected to demonstrate mastery of the central algebraic operations, including proper usage of exponents in problem-solving and understanding how to both factor and expand polynomials. In addition, you will be expected to understand absolute value as well as how to apply operations in algebraic expressions. Finally, you must demonstrate a sound understanding of logarithms and their properties.

To demonstrate mastery of equations and inequalities, you must be able to both understand and create accurate equations and inequalities, including those that are linear, quadratic, or involve absolute value. You must also be able to solve problems involving system of equations and inequalities, as well as those involving exponential and logarithmic equations.

You also must have a strong grasp of the properties of algebraic functions. You must be able to define and interpret the various functions as well as represent them in a variety of ways, including graphically, numerically, symbolically, and verbally. You must be able to determine domain and range, apply the algebra of functions, properly utilize inverse functions, and interpret graphs and determine their properties, including intercepts, symmetry, and transformations.

In addition to understanding algebraic functions, you must demonstrate mastery of number systems, including both real and complex numbers. You must also be able to identify and interpret sequences and series, properly solve factorials, and apply the binomial theorem.

How is the CLEP College Algebra Exam Scored?

You will receive your scores on your CLEP College Algebra Exam immediately upon your completion of the exam. At the end of the test, you will have the option not to have your test scored. If you do not want your scores reported, select this option. It is important to note that you must make this choice BEFORE you have seen your score. Once you have seen your score, you cannot choose to have it cancelled.

Your CLEP scores will automatically be added to your CLEP transcript. When you register, you can pre-select the college or employer you would like to receive your scores. If you are taking the exam before you have decided where you are attending school, you can request your CLEP transcript when you are ready. The first transcript request is free regardless of when it is requested.

Each multiple-choice question is worth one raw point. The total number of questions you answer correctly is added up to obtain your raw score. The raw score is then scaled to a score between twenty and eighty. Minimum passing scores vary by institution, so check with your college or university.

There is no guessing penalty on the CLEP College Algebra exam, so you should always guess if you do not know the answer to a question.

How is the CLEP College Algebra Exam Administered?

The CLEP College Algebra exam is a computer-based test offered at over 1,800 locations worldwide. There are four different types of test centers:

- Open test centers will test any student who has registered and paid the fee.
- Limited test centers are located at universities and colleges and will only test admitted or enrolled students.
- On-base test centers are located in military installations and only test eligible service members and civilians with authorized access to the installation.
- Fully-funded test centers are also only for military service members, eligible civilians, and their spouses. These centers test DANTES-funded test-takers who are exempt from the administrative fee.

Regardless of the type of test center, you must contact the test center directly to make a reservation to take the exam. Check https://clep.collegeboard.org/search/test-centers for more information.

You will need to print your registration ticket from your online account and bring it, along with your identification, to the testing site on exam day. Some test centers will require other forms or documentation, so check with your test center in advance. Test centers may also require administrative fees in addition to the registration fee for the exam itself. No pens, pencils, erasers, printed or written materials, electronic devices, or calculators are allowed. An online scientific calculator will be provided to you at the time of the test. You can access the calculator for free for thirty days before your test in order to familiarize yourself with it.

You may not bring a bag with you into the testing room. You are also forbidden to wear headwear (unless for religious purposes). You may take the test once every three months. Please note that DANTES does not fund retesting.

About This Guide

This guide will help you master the most important test topics and also develop critical test-taking skills. We have built features into our books to prepare you for your tests and increase your score. Along with a detailed summary of the test's format, content, and scoring, we offer an in-depth overview of the content knowledge required to pass the test. In the content review sections, you'll find sidebars that provide interesting information, highlight key concepts, and review content so that you can solidify your understanding of the material you will be tested on. You can also test your knowledge with sample questions throughout the text and practice questions that reflect the content and format of the CLEP College Algebra exam. We're pleased you've chosen Accepted, Inc. to be a part of your college journey!

one

NUMBER SYSTEMS AND OPERATIONS

This chapter provides a review of the basic yet critical components of mathematics such as manipulating fractions, comparing numbers, and using units. These concepts will provide the foundation for more complex mathematical operations in later chapters.

Types of Numbers

Numbers are placed in categories based on their properties.

- A **NATURAL NUMBER** is greater than 0 and has no decimal or fraction attached. These are also sometimes called counting numbers {1, 2, 3, 4, ...}.

- **WHOLE NUMBERS** are natural numbers and the number 0 {0, 1, 2, 3, 4, ...}.

- **INTEGERS** include positive and negative natural numbers and 0 {..., –4, –3, –2, –1, 0, 1, 2, 3, 4, ...}.

- A **RATIONAL NUMBER** can be represented as a fraction. Any decimal part must terminate or resolve into a repeating pattern. Examples include –12, $-\frac{4}{5}$, 0.36, $7.\overline{7}$, $26\frac{1}{2}$, etc.

- An **IRRATIONAL NUMBER** cannot be represented as a fraction. An irrational decimal number never ends and never resolves into a repeating pattern. Examples include $-\sqrt{7}$, π, and 0.34567989135...

- A **REAL NUMBER** is a number that can be represented by a point on a number line. Real numbers include all the rational and irrational numbers.

- An **IMAGINARY NUMBER** includes the imaginary unit i, where $i = \sqrt{-1}$ Because $i^2 = -1$, imaginary numbers produce a negative value when squared. Examples of imaginary numbers include $-4i$, $0.75i$, $i\sqrt{2}$ and $\frac{8}{3}i$.

◆ A **COMPLEX NUMBER** is in the form $a + bi$, where a and b are real numbers. Examples of complex numbers include $3 + 2i$, $-4 + i$, $\sqrt{3} - i\sqrt[3]{5}$ and $\frac{5}{8} - \frac{7i}{8}$. All imaginary numbers are also complex.

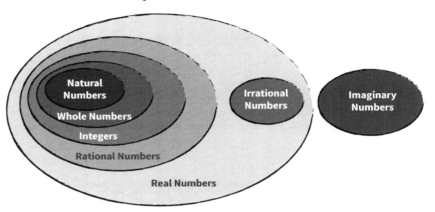

Figure 1.1. Types of Numbers

The **FACTORS** of a natural number are all the numbers that can multiply together to make the number. For example, the factors of 24 are 1, 2, 3, 4, 6, 8, 12, and 24. Every natural number is either prime or composite. A **PRIME NUMBER** is a number that is only divisible by itself and 1. (The number 1 is not considered prime.) Examples of prime numbers are 2, 3, 7, and 29. The number 2 is the only even prime number. A **COMPOSITE NUMBER** has more than two factors. For example, 6 is composite because its factors are 1, 6, 2, and 3. Every composite number can be written as a unique product of prime numbers, called the **PRIME FACTORIZATION** of the number. For example, the prime factorization of 90 is $90 = 2 \times 3^2 \times 5$. All integers are either even or odd. An even number is divisible by 2; an odd number is not.

If a real number is a natural number (e.g., 50), then it is also a whole number, an integer, and a rational number.

EXAMPLES

1) Classify the following numbers as natural, whole, integer, rational, or irrational. (The numbers may have more than one classification.)

   A. 72

   B. $-\frac{2}{3}$

   C. $\sqrt{5}$

   Answers:

   A. The number is **natural**, **whole**, an **integer**, and **rational**.

   B. The fraction is **rational**.

C. The number is **irrational**. (It cannot be written as a fraction, and written as a decimal is approximately 2.2360679...)

2) Determine the real and imaginary parts of the following complex numbers.

   A. 20

   B. $10 - i$

   C. $15i$

Answers:

A complex number is in the form of $a + bi$, where a is the real part and bi is the imaginary part.

A. $20 = 20 + 0i$

The real part is 20, and there is no imaginary part.

B. $10 - i = 10 - 1i$

The real part is 10, and $-1i$ is the imaginary part.

C. $15i = 0 + 15i$

The real part is 0, and the imaginary part is $15i$.

Properties of Number Systems

A system is CLOSED under an operation if performing that operation on two elements of the system results in another element of that system. For example, the integers are closed under the operations of addition, subtraction, and multiplication but not division. Adding, subtracting, or multiplying two integers results in another integer. However, dividing two integers could result in a rational number that is not an integer $\left(-2 \div 3 = \frac{-2}{3} \right)$.

▸ The rational numbers are closed under all four operations (except for division by 0).

▸ The real numbers are closed under all four operations.

▸ The complex numbers are closed under all four operations.

▸ The irrational numbers are NOT closed under ANY of the four operations.

The COMMUTATIVE PROPERTY holds for an operation if order does not matter when performing the operation. For example, multiplication is commutative for integers: $(-2)(3) = (3)(-2)$.

The ASSOCIATIVE PROPERTY holds for an operation if elements can be regrouped without changing the result. For example, addition is associative for real numbers: $-3 + (-5 + 4) = (-3 + -5) + 4$.

The DISTRIBUTIVE PROPERTY of multiplication over addition allows a product of sums to be written as a sum of products: $a(b + c) = ab + ac$. The value a is distributed over the sum $(b + c)$. The acronym FOIL

(First, Outer, Inner, Last) is a useful way to remember the distributive property.

When an operation is performed with an IDENTITY ELEMENT and another element a, the result is a. The identity element for multiplication on real numbers is 1 ($a \times 1 = a$), and for addition is 0 ($a + 0 = a$).

An operation of a system has an INVERSE ELEMENT if applying that operation with the inverse element results in the identity element. For example, the inverse element of a for addition is $-a$ because $a + (-a) = 0$. The inverse element of a for multiplication is $\frac{1}{a}$ because $a \times \frac{1}{a} = 1$.

EXAMPLES

1) Classify the following numbers as natural, whole, integer, rational, or irrational. (The numbers may have more than one classification.)

   A. 72

   B. $-\frac{2}{3}$

   C. $\sqrt{5}$

   Answers:

   A. The number is **natural**, **whole**, an **integer**, and **rational**.

   B. The fraction is **rational**.

   C. The number is **irrational**. (It cannot be written as a fraction, and written as a decimal is approximately 2.2360679...)

2) Determine the real and imaginary parts of the following complex numbers.

   A. 20

   B. $10 - i$

   C. $15i$

   Answers:

   A complex number is in the form of $a + bi$, where a is the real part and bi is the imaginary part.

   A. $20 = 20 + 0i$
   The real part is 20, and there is no imaginary part.

   B. $10 - i = 10 - 1i$
   The real part is 10, and $-1i$ is the imaginary part.

   C. $15i = 0 + 15i$
   The real part is 0, and the imaginary part is $15i$.

3) Answer True or False for each statement:

A. The natural numbers are closed under subtraction.

B. The sum of two irrational numbers is irrational.

C. The sum of a rational number and an irrational number is irrational.

Answers:

A. **False**. Subtracting the natural number 7 from 2 results in $2 - 7 = -5$, which is an integer, but not a natural number.

B. **False**. For example, $(5 - 2\sqrt{3}) + (2 + 2\sqrt{3}) = 7$. The sum of two irrational numbers in this example is a whole number, which is not irrational. The sum of a rational number and an irrational number is sometimes rational and sometimes irrational.

C. **True**. Because irrational numbers have decimal parts that are unending and with no pattern, adding a repeating or terminating decimal will still result in an unending decimal without a pattern.

4) Answer True or False for each statement:

A. The associative property applies for multiplication in the real numbers.

B. The commutative property applies to all real numbers and all operations.

Answers:

A. **True**. For all real numbers, $a \times (b \times c) = (a \times b) \times c$. Order of multiplication does not change the result.

B. **False**. The commutative property does not work for subtraction or division on real numbers. For example, $12 - 5 = 7$, but $5 - 12 = -7$ and $10 \div 2 = 5$, but $2 \div 10 = \frac{1}{5}$.

Operations with Complex Numbers

Operations with complex numbers are similar to operations with real numbers in that complex numbers can be added, subtracted, multiplied, and divided. When adding or subtracting, the imaginary parts and real parts are combined separately. When multiplying, the distributive property (FOIL) can be applied. Note that multiplying complex numbers often creates the value i^2 which can be simplified to -1.

To divide complex numbers, multiply both the top and bottom of the fraction by the COMPLEX CONJUGATE of the divisor (bottom number). The complex conjugate is the complex number with the sign of the imaginary part changed. For example, the complex conjugate of $3 + 4i$ would be $3 - 4i$. Since both the top and the bottom of the fraction are multiplied by the same number, the fraction is really just being multiplied by 1. When simplified, the denominator of the fraction will now be a real number.

EXAMPLES

1) Simplify: $(3 - 2i) - (-2 + 8i)$

Answer:

$(3 - 2i) - (-2 + 8i)$

$= (3 - 2i) - 1(-2 + 8i)$ | Distribute the −1.

$= 3 - 2i + 2 - 8i$

$= \mathbf{5 - 10i}$ | Combine like terms.

2) Simplify: $\dfrac{4i}{(5 - 2i)}$

Answer:

$\dfrac{4i}{(5 - 2i)}$

$= \dfrac{4i}{5 - 2i}\left(\dfrac{5 + 2i}{5 + 2i}\right)$ | Multiply the top and bottom of the fraction by the complex conjugate of $5 + 2i$.

$= \dfrac{20i + 8i^2}{25 + 10i - 10i - 4i^2}$

$= \dfrac{20i + 8(-1)}{25 + 10i - 10i - 4(-1)}$ | Simplify the result using the identity $i^2 = -1$.

$= \dfrac{20i - 8}{25 + 10i - 10i + 4}$

$= \dfrac{20i - 8}{29}$ | Combine like terms.

$= \dfrac{-8}{29} + \dfrac{20}{29}i$ | Write the answer in the form $a + bi$.

Figure 1.2. Scientific Notation

$65000000.$

$7\ 6\ 5\ 4\ 3\ 2\ 1$

6.5×10^7

$.0000987$

$-1\text{-}2\text{-}3\text{-}4\text{-}5$

9.87×10^{-5}

When multiplying numbers in scientific notation, add the exponents. When dividing, subtract the exponents.

Scientific Notation

SCIENTIFIC NOTATION is a method of representing very large and small numbers in the form $a \times 10^n$, where a is a value between 1 and 10, and n is a nonzero integer. For example, the number 927,000,000 is written in scientific notation as 9.27×10^8. Multiplying 9.27 by 10 eight times gives 927,000,000. When performing operations with scientific notation, the final answer should be in the form $a \times 10^n$.

When adding and subtracting numbers in scientific notation, the power of 10 must be the same for all numbers. This results in like terms in which the a terms are added or subtracted and the 10^n remains unchanged. When multiplying numbers in scientific notation, multiply the a factors, and then multiply that answer by 10 to the sum of the exponents. For division, divide the a factors and subtract the exponents.

EXAMPLES

1) Simplify: $(3.8 \times 10^3) + (4.7 \times 10^2)$

Answer:

$(3.8 \times 10^3) + (4.7 \times 10^2)$	
$3.8 \times 10^3 = 3.8 \times 10 \times 10^2 = 38 \times 10^2$	To add, the exponents of 10 must be the same.
$38 \times 10^2 + 4.7 \times 10^2 = 42.7 \times 10^2$	Add the a terms together.
$\mathbf{= 4.27 \times 10^3}$	Write the number in proper scientific notation.

2) Simplify: $(8.1 \times 10^{-5})(1.4 \times 10^7)$

Answer:

$(8.1 \times 10^{-5})(1.4 \times 10^7)$	
$8.1 \times 1.4 = 11.34$	Multiply the a factors and add the exponents on the base of 10.
$-5 + 7 = 2$	
$= 11.34 \times 10^2$	
$\mathbf{= 1.134 \times 10^3}$	Write the number in proper scientific notation.

Order of Operations

The **order of operations** is simply the order in which operations are performed. **PEMDAS** is a common way to remember the order of operations:

1.	Parentheses		**4.**	Division
2.	Exponents		**5.**	Addition
3.	Multiplication		**6.**	Subtraction

Multiplication and division, and addition and subtraction, are performed together from left to right. So, performing multiple operations on a set of numbers is a four-step process:

1. P: Calculate expressions inside parentheses, brackets, braces, etc.
2. E: Calculate exponents and square roots.
3. MD: Calculate any remaining multiplication and division in order from left to right.
4. AS: Calculate any remaining addition and subtraction in order from left to right.

Always work from left to right within each step when simplifying expressions.

EXAMPLES

1) Simplify: $2(21 - 14) + 6 \div (-2) \times 3 - 10$

Answer:

$2(21 - 14) + 6 \div (-2) \times 3 - 10$	
$= 2(7) + 6 \div (-2) \times 3 - 10$	Calculate expressions inside parentheses.
$= 14 + 6 \div (-2) \times 3 - 10$	There are no exponents or radicals, so perform multiplication and division from left to right.
$= 14 + (-3) \times 3 - 10$	
$= 14 + (-9) - 10$	
$= 5 - 10$	Perform addition and subtraction from left to right.
$= \mathbf{-5}$	

2) Simplify: $-(3)^2 + 4(5) + (5 - 6)^2 - 8$

Answer:

$-(3)^2 + 4(5) + (5 - 6)^2 - 8$	
$= -(3)^2 + 4(5) + (-1)^2 - 8$	Calculate expressions inside parentheses.
$= -9 + 4(5) + 1 - 8$	Simplify exponents and radicals.
$= -9 + 20 + 1 - 8$	Perform multiplication and division from left to right.
$= 11 + 1 - 8$	
$= 12 - 8$	Perform addition and subtraction from left to right.
$= \mathbf{4}$	

3) Simplify: $\dfrac{(7 - 9)^3 + 8(10 - 12)}{4^2 - 5^2}$

Answer:

$\dfrac{(7 - 9)^3 + 8(10 - 12)}{4^2 - 5^2}$	
$= \dfrac{(-2)^3 + 8(-2)}{4^2 - 5^2}$	Calculate expressions inside parentheses.
$= \dfrac{-8 + (-16)}{16 - 25}$	Simplify exponents and radicals.
$= \dfrac{-24}{-9}$	Perform addition and subtraction from left to right.
$= \dfrac{\mathbf{8}}{\mathbf{3}}$	Simplify.

Fractions

A **FRACTION** is a number that can be written in the form $\frac{a}{b}$, where b is not equal to 0. The a part of the fraction is the **NUMERATOR** (top number) and the b part of the fraction is the **DENOMINATOR** (bottom number).

If the denominator of a fraction is greater than the numerator, the value of the fraction is less than 1 and it is called a **PROPER FRACTION** (for example, $\frac{3}{5}$ is a proper fraction). In an **IMPROPER FRACTION**, the denominator is less than the numerator and the value of the fraction is greater than 1 ($\frac{8}{3}$ is an improper fraction). An improper fraction can be written as a **MIXED NUMBER**, which has a whole number part and a proper fraction part. Improper fractions can be converted to mixed numbers by dividing the numerator by the denominator, which gives the whole number part, and the remainder becomes the numerator of the proper fraction part. (For example, the improper fraction $\frac{25}{9}$ is equal to mixed number $2\frac{7}{9}$ because 9 divides into 25 two times, with a remainder of 7.)

Conversely, mixed numbers can be converted to improper fractions. To do so, determine the numerator of the improper fraction by multiplying the denominator by the whole number, and then adding the numerator. The final number is written as the (now larger) numerator over the original denominator.

To convert mixed numbers to improper fractions:

$$a\frac{m}{n} = \frac{n \times a + m}{n}$$

Fractions with the same denominator can be added or subtracted by simply adding or subtracting the numerators; the denominator will remain unchanged. To add or subtract fractions with different denominators, find the **LEAST COMMON DENOMINATOR (LCD)** of all the fractions. The LCD is the smallest number exactly divisible by each denominator. (For example, the least common denominator of the numbers 2, 3, and 8 is 24.) Once the LCD has been found, each fraction should be written in an equivalent form with the LCD as the denominator.

$$\frac{a}{b} \pm \frac{c}{b} = \frac{a \pm c}{b}$$
$$\frac{a}{b} \times \frac{c}{d} = \frac{ac}{bd}$$
$$\frac{a}{b} \div \frac{c}{d} = \left(\frac{a}{b}\right)\left(\frac{d}{c}\right) = \frac{ad}{bc}$$

To multiply fractions, the numerators are multiplied together and denominators are multiplied together. If there are any mixed numbers, they should first be changed to improper fractions. Then, the numerators are multiplied together and the denominators are multiplied together. The fraction can then be reduced if necessary. To divide fractions, multiply the first fraction by the reciprocal of the second.

Any common denominator can be used to add or subtract fractions. The quickest way to find a common denominator of a set of values is simply to multiply all the values together. The result might not be the least common denominator, but it will allow the problem to be worked.

EXAMPLES

1) Simplify: $2\frac{3}{5} + 3\frac{1}{4} - 1\frac{1}{2}$

Answer:

$2\frac{3}{5} + 3\frac{1}{4} - 1\frac{1}{2}$

$= 2\frac{12}{20} + 3\frac{5}{20} - 1\frac{10}{20}$

Change each fraction so it has a denominator of 20, which is the LCD of 5, 4, and 2.

$2 + 3 - 1 = 4$

$\frac{12}{20} + \frac{5}{20} - \frac{10}{20} = \frac{7}{20}$

Add and subtract the whole numbers together and the fractions together.

$4\frac{7}{20}$

Combine to get the final answer (a mixed number).

2) Simplify: $\frac{7}{8} \times 3\frac{1}{3}$

Answer:

$\frac{7}{8} \times 3\frac{1}{3}$

$3\frac{1}{3} = \frac{10}{3}$

Change the mixed number to an improper fraction.

$\frac{7}{8}\left(\frac{10}{3}\right) = \frac{7 \times 10}{8 \times 3}$

$= \frac{70}{24}$

Multiply the numerators together and the denominators together.

$= \frac{35}{12}$

Reduce the fraction.

$= 2\frac{11}{12}$

3) Simplify: $4\frac{1}{2} \div \frac{2}{3}$

Answer:

$4\frac{1}{2} \div \frac{2}{3}$

$4\frac{1}{2} = \frac{9}{2}$

Change the mixed number to an improper fraction.

$\frac{9}{2} \div \frac{2}{3}$

$= \frac{9}{2} \times \frac{3}{2}$

Multiply the first fraction by the reciprocal of the second fraction.

$= \frac{27}{4}$

$= 6\frac{3}{4}$

Simplify.

Ratios

A RATIO is a comparison of two numbers and can be represented as $\frac{a}{b}$, $a:b$, or a to b. The two numbers represent a constant relationship, not a specific value: for every a number of items in the first group, there will be b number of items in the second. For example, if the ratio of blue to red candies in a bag is 3:5, the bag will contain 3 blue candies for every 5 red candies. So, the bag might contain 3 blue candies and 5 red candies, or it might contain 30 blue candies and 50 red candies, or 36 blue candies and 60 red candies. All of these values are representative of the ratio 3:5 (which is the ratio in its lowest, or simplest, terms).

To find the "whole" when working with ratios, simply add the values in the ratio. For example, if the ratio of boys to girls in a class is 2:3, the "whole" is five: 2 out of every 5 students are boys, and 3 out of every 5 students are girls.

EXAMPLES

1) There are 10 boys and 12 girls in a first-grade class. What is the ratio of boys to the total number of students? What is the ratio of girls to boys?

   Answer:

number of boys: 10 number of girls: 12 number of students: 22	Identify the variables.
number of boys : number of students $= 10 : 22$ $= \frac{10}{22}$ $= \frac{5}{11}$	Write out and simplify the ratio of boys to total students.
number of girls : number of boys $= 12 : 10$ $= \frac{12}{10}$ $= \frac{6}{5}$	Write out and simplify the ratio of girls to boys.

2) A family spends $600 a month on rent, $400 on utilities, $750 on groceries, and $550 on miscellaneous expenses. What is the ratio of the family's rent to their total expenses?

   Answer:

rent = 600	
utilities = 400	
groceries = 750	Identify the variables.
miscellaneous = 550	
total expenses = 600 + 400 + 750 + 550 = 2300	
rent : total expenses	
= 600 : 2300	Write out and simplify the ratio of rent to total expenses.
$= \frac{600}{2300}$	
$= \frac{6}{23}$	

Proportions

A **PROPORTION** is an equation which states that two ratios are equal. A proportion is given in the form $\frac{a}{b} = \frac{c}{d}$, where the a and d terms are the extremes and the b and c terms are the means. A proportion is solved using cross-multiplication ($ad = bc$) to create an equation with no fractional components. A proportion must have the same units in both numerators and both denominators.

EXAMPLES

1) Solve the proportion for x: $\frac{3x-5}{2} = \frac{x-8}{3}$.

   Answer:

$\frac{(3x-5)}{2} = \frac{(x-8)}{3}$	
$3(3x-5) = 2(x-8)$	Cross-multiply.
$9x - 15 = 2x - 16$	
$7x - 15 = -16$	
$7x = -1$	Solve the equation for x.
$x = -\frac{1}{7}$	

2) A map is drawn such that 2.5 inches on the map equates to an actual distance of 40 miles. If the distance measured on the map between two cities is 17.25 inches, what is the actual distance between them in miles?

   Answer:

$\frac{2.5}{40} = \frac{17.25}{x}$	Write a proportion where x equals the actual distance and each ratio is written as inches : miles.

$2.5x = 690$

$x = 276$

The two cities are **276 miles apart**.

| Cross-multiply and divide to solve for x.

3) A factory knows that 4 out of 1000 parts made will be defective. If in a month there are 125,000 parts made, how many of these parts will be defective?

Answer:

$$\frac{4}{1000} = \frac{x}{125,000}$$

Write a proportion where x is the number of defective parts made and both ratios are written as defective : total.

$1000x = 500,000$

$x = 500$

There are **500 defective parts** for the month.

Cross-multiply and divide to solve for x.

Answer:

original amount = $100,000

amount of change = 120,000 − 100,000 = 20,000

percent change = ?

Identify the variables.

$$\text{percent change} = \frac{\text{amount of change}}{\text{original amount}}$$
$$= \frac{20,000}{100,000}$$
$$= 0.20$$

Plug the variables into the appropriate equation.

$0.20 \times 100 =$ **20%**

To find the percent growth, multiply by 100.

Exponents and Radicals

Exponents

An expression in the form b^n is in an exponential notation where b is the BASE and n is an EXPONENT. To perform the operation, multiply the base by itself the number of times indicated by the exponent. For example, 2^3 is equal to $2 \times 2 \times 2$ or 8.

Table 1.1. Operations with Exponents

RULE	EXAMPLE	EXPLANATION
$a^0 = 1$	$5^0 = 1$	Any base (except 0) to the 0 power is 1.
$a^n = \frac{1}{a^n}$	$5^3 = \frac{1}{5^3}$	A negative exponent becomes positive when moved from numerator to denominator (or vice versa).
$a^m a^n = a^{m+n}$	$5^3 5^4 = 5^{3+4} = 5^7$	Add the exponents to multiply two powers with the same base.
$(a^m)^n$	$(5^3)^4 = 5^{3(4)} = 5^{12}$	Multiply the exponents to raise a power to a power.
$\frac{a^m}{a^n} = a^{m-n}$	$\frac{5^4}{5^3} = 5^{4-3} = 5^1$	Subtract the exponents to divide two powers with the same base.
$(ab)^n = a^n b^n$	$(5 \times 6)^3 = 5^3 6^3$	Apply the exponent to each base to raise a product to a power.
$\frac{a}{b}^n = \frac{a^n}{b^n}$	$\frac{(5/6)^3}{6} = \frac{5^3}{6^3}$	Apply the exponent to each base to raise a quotient to a power.
$\frac{(a/b)^{-n}}{b} = \frac{b}{a}$	$\frac{(5/6)^{-3}}{6} = \frac{(6/5)^3}{5}$	Invert the fraction and change the sign of the exponent to raise a fraction to a negative power.
$\frac{a^m}{b^n} = \frac{(b/a)^n}{a^m}$	$\frac{5^3}{6^4} = \frac{6^4}{5^3}$	Change the sign of the exponent when moving a number from the numerator to denominator (or vice versa).

EXAMPLES

1) Simplify: $\frac{(10^2)^3}{(10^2)^2}$

   Answer:

   $\frac{(10^2)^3}{(10^2)^2}$

   $= \frac{10^6}{10^{-4}}$ Multiply the exponents raised to a power.

   $= 10^{6-(-4)}$ Subtract the exponent in the denominator from the one in the numerator.

   $= 10^{10}$ Simplify.

   $= \mathbf{10,000,000,000}$

2) Simplify: $\frac{(x^{-2}y^2)^2}{x^3y}$

   Answer:

   $\frac{(x^{-2}y^2)^2}{x^3y}$

   $= \frac{x^{-4}y^4}{x^3y}$ Multiply the exponents raised to a power.

$= x^{-4-3}y^{4-1}$	Subtract the exponent in the denominator from the one in the numerator.
$= x^{-7}y^3$	
$= \dfrac{y^3}{x^7}$	Move negative exponents to the denominator.

Radicals

RADICALS are expressed as $\sqrt[b]{a}$, where b is called the INDEX and a is the RADICAND. A radical is used to indicate the inverse operation of an exponent: finding the base which can be raised to b to yield a. For example, $\sqrt[3]{125}$ is equal to 5 because $5 \times 5 \times 5$ equals 125. The same operation can be expressed using a fraction exponent, so $\sqrt[b]{a} = \dfrac{1}{a^b}$. Note that when no value is indicated for b, it is assumed to be 2 (square root).

When b is even and a is positive, $\sqrt[b]{a}$ is defined to be the positive real value n such that $n^b = a$ (example: $\sqrt{16} = 4$ only, and not -4, even though $(-4)(-4) = 16$). If b is even and a is negative, $\sqrt[b]{a}$ will be a complex number (example: $\sqrt{-9} = 3i$). Finally if b is odd, $\sqrt[b]{a}$ will always be a real number regardless of the sign of a. If a is negative, $\sqrt[b]{a}$ will be negative since a number to an odd power is negative (example: $\sqrt[5]{-32} = -2$ since $(-2)^5 = -32$).

$\sqrt[n]{x}$ is referred to as the nth root of x.

- ◆ $n = 2$ is the square root
- ◆ $n = 3$ is the cube root
- ◆ $n = 4$ is the fourth root
- ◆ $n = 5$ is the fifth root

The following table of operations with radicals holds for all cases EXCEPT the case where b is even and a is negative (the complex case).

Table 1.3. Operations with Radicals

RULE	EXAMPLE	EXPLANATION
$\sqrt[b]{ac} = \sqrt[b]{a}\,\sqrt[b]{c}$	$\sqrt[3]{81} = \sqrt[3]{27}\,\sqrt[3]{3} = 3\sqrt[3]{3}$	The values under the radical sign can be separated into values that multiply to the original value.
$\sqrt[b]{\dfrac{a}{c}} = \dfrac{\sqrt[b]{a}}{\sqrt[b]{c}}$	$\sqrt{\dfrac{4}{81}} = \dfrac{\sqrt{4}}{\sqrt{81}} = \dfrac{2}{9}$	The b-root of the numerator and denominator can be calculated when there is a fraction under a radical sign.
$\sqrt[b]{a^c} = (\sqrt[b]{a})^c = a^{\frac{c}{b}}$	$\sqrt[3]{6^2} = (\sqrt[3]{6})^2 = 6^{\frac{2}{3}}$	The b-root can be written as a fractional exponent. If there is a power under the radical sign, it will be the numerator of the fraction.

$$\frac{c}{\sqrt[b]{a}} \times \frac{\sqrt[b]{a}}{\sqrt[b]{a}} = \frac{c\sqrt[b]{a}}{a} \qquad \frac{5}{\sqrt{2}} \frac{\sqrt{2}}{\sqrt{2}} = \frac{5\sqrt{2}}{2}$$

To rationalize the denominator, multiply the numerator and denominator by the radical in the denominator until the radical has been canceled out.

$$\frac{c}{b-\sqrt{a}} \times \frac{b+\sqrt{a}}{b+\sqrt{a}} \qquad \frac{4}{3-\sqrt{2}} \frac{3+\sqrt{2}}{3+\sqrt{2}}$$

$$= \frac{c(b+\sqrt{a})}{b^2-a} \qquad = \frac{4(3+\sqrt{2})}{9-2} = \frac{12+4\sqrt{2}}{7}$$

To rationalize the denominator, the numerator and denominator are multiplied by the conjugate of the denominator.

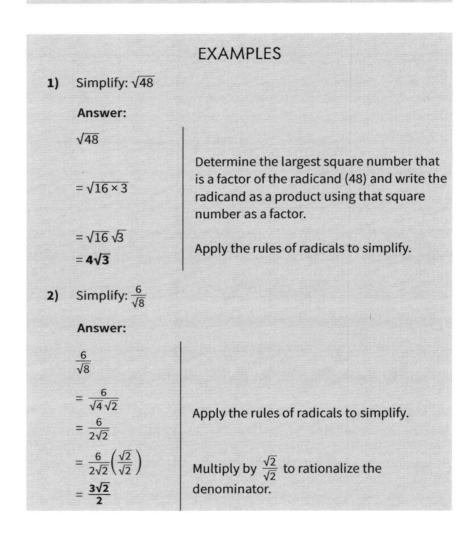

EXAMPLES

1) Simplify: $\sqrt{48}$

   Answer:

   $\sqrt{48}$

   $= \sqrt{16 \times 3}$

   Determine the largest square number that is a factor of the radicand (48) and write the radicand as a product using that square number as a factor.

   $= \sqrt{16}\sqrt{3}$

   $= \mathbf{4\sqrt{3}}$

   Apply the rules of radicals to simplify.

2) Simplify: $\frac{6}{\sqrt{8}}$

   Answer:

   $\frac{6}{\sqrt{8}}$

   $= \frac{6}{\sqrt{4}\sqrt{2}}$

   Apply the rules of radicals to simplify.

   $= \frac{6}{2\sqrt{2}}$

   $= \frac{6}{2\sqrt{2}}\left(\frac{\sqrt{2}}{\sqrt{2}}\right)$

   Multiply by $\frac{\sqrt{2}}{\sqrt{2}}$ to rationalize the denominator.

   $= \mathbf{\frac{3\sqrt{2}}{2}}$

Sequences and Series

Sequences can be thought of as a set of numbers (called TERMS) with a rule that explains the particular pattern between the terms. The terms of a sequence are separated by commas. There are two types of sequences that will be examined, arithmetic and geometric. The sum of an arithmetic sequence is known as an ARITHMETIC SERIES; similarly the sum of a geometric sequence is known as a GEOMETRIC SERIES.

Arithmetic Sequences

ARITHMETIC GROWTH is constant growth, meaning that the difference between any one term in the series and the next consecutive term will be the same constant. This constant is called the COMMON DIFFERENCE. Thus, to list the terms in the sequence, one can just add (or subtract) the same number repeatedly. For example, the series {20, 30, 40, 50} is arithmetic since 10 is added each time to get from one term to the next. One way to represent this sequence is using a RECURSIVE definition, which basically says: *next term = current term + common difference*. For this example, the recursive definition would be $a_{n+1} = a_n + 10$ because the *next* term a_{n+1} in the sequence is the current term a_n plus 10. In general, the recursive definition of a series is:

$a_{n+1} = a_n + d$, where d is the common difference.

Often, the objective of arithmetic sequence questions is to find a specific term in the sequence or the sum of a certain series of terms. The formulas to use are:

Table 1.2. Formulas for Arithmetic Sequences and Series

FINDING THE *N*TH TERM . . .

	d = the common difference of the sequence
	a_n = the nth term in the sequence
$a_n = a_1 + d(n-1)$	n = the number of the term
$a_n = a_m + d(n-m)$	a_m = the mth term in the sequence
	m = the number of the term
	a_1 = the first term in the sequence

FINDING THE PARTIAL SUM . . .

	S_n = sum of the terms through the nth term
$S_n = \dfrac{n(a_1 + a_n)}{2}$	a_n = the nth term in the sequence
	n = the number of the term
	a_1 = the first term in the sequence

EXAMPLES

1) Find the ninth term of the sequence: −57, −40, −23, −6 …

Answer:

$a_1 = -57$	
$d = -57 - (-40) = 17$	Identify the variables given.
$n = 9$	
$a_9 = -57 + 17(9-1)$	Plug these values into the formula for the specific term of an arithmetic sequence.

$a_9 = -57 + 17(8)$

$a_9 = -57 + 136$

$a_9 = 79$ | Solve for a_9.

2) If the 23rd term in an arithmetic sequence is 820, and the 5th term is 200, find the common difference between each term.

Answer:

$a_5 = 200$	
$a_{23} = 820$	
$n = 23$	Idenfity the variables given.
$m = 5$	
$d = ?$	
$a_n = a_m + d(n - m)$	Plug these values into the
$820 = 200 + d(23 - 5)$	equation for using one term to
$620 = d(18)$	find another in an arithmetic
$d = 34.\overline{44}$	sequence.

3) Evaluate $\sum_{n=14}^{45} 2n + 10$.

Answer:

$a_1 = 2(1) + 10 = 12$	
$n = 45$	
$a_n = 2(45) + 10 = 100$	Find the partial sum of the first
$S_n = \dfrac{n(a_1 + a_n)}{2}$	45 terms.
$= \dfrac{45(12 + 100)}{2}$	
$= 2520$	
$a_1 = 2(1) + 10 = 12$	
$n = 13$	
$a_n = 2(13) + 10 = 36$	Find the partial sum of the first
$S_n = \dfrac{n(a_1 + a_n)}{2}$	13 terms.
$= \dfrac{13(12 + 36)}{2}$	
$= 312$	
$S_{45} - S_{13} = 2520 - 312$	The sum of the terms between
$= 2208$	14 and 45 will be the difference between S_{45} and S_{13}.

Geometric Sequences

While an arithmetic sequence has an additive pattern, a GEOMETRIC SEQUENCE has a multiplicative pattern. This means that to get from any one term in the sequence to the next term in the sequence, the term is multiplied by a fixed number (called the COMMON RATIO). The following sequence is a geometric sequence: {8, 4, 2, 1, .5, .25, .125}. In this case, the multiplier (or common ratio) is $\frac{1}{2}$. The multiplier can be any real number other than 0 or 1. To find the common ratio, simply choose any term in the sequence and divide it by the previous term (this is the ratio of two consecutive terms—thus the name common *ratio*). In the above example, the ratio between the second and third terms is $\frac{2}{4} = \frac{1}{2}$.

Geometric sequences require their own formulas to find the next term and a sum of a specific series.

> Compared to arithmetic growth, geometric growth is much faster. As seen in the formulas used to find a geometric term, geometric growth is exponential, whereas arithmetic growth is linear.

Table 1.3. Geometric Sequences: Formulas

FINDING THE NTH TERM . . .

$a_n = a_1 \times r^{n-1}$ $a_n = a_m \times r^{n-m}$	r = the common ratio of the sequence a_n = the nth term in the sequence n = the number of the term a_m = the mth term in the sequence m = the number of the term a_1 = the first term in the sequence

FINDING THE PARTIAL SUM . . .

$S_n = \dfrac{a_1(1 - r^n)}{1 - r}$	S_n = sum of the terms through the nth term r = the common ratio of the sequence a_n = the nth term in the sequence n = the number of the term a_1 = the first term in the sequence

FINDING THE SUM OF AN INFINITE SERIES . . .

$S_\infty = \dfrac{a}{1 - r}$ ($\lvert r \rvert < 1$)	S_∞ = sum of all terms r = the common ratio of the sequence a = the fifth term in the sequence

The finite sum formula works similarly to the arithmetic sequence sum. However, sometimes the INFINITE SUM of the sequence must be found. The sum of an infinite number of terms of a sequence is called a SERIES. If the infinite terms of the sequence add up to a finite number, the series is said to CONVERGE to that number. If the sum of the terms is infinite, then the series DIVERGES. Another way to say this is to ask: is there a limit to the finite sum S_n as n goes to infinity? For geometric series in the form $\sum_{n=1}^{\infty} a \times r^n$, the series converges only when $\lvert r \rvert < 1$

(or –1 < r < 1). If r is greater than 1, the sum will approach infinity, so the series diverges.

EXAMPLES

57) Find the 8th term in the sequence: {13, 39, 117, 351 . . .}

Answer:

$a_1 = 13$	
$n = 8$	Identify the variables given.
$r = \frac{39}{13} = 3$	
$a_8 = 13 \times 3^{8-1}$	Plug these values into the equation to find a specific term in a geometric sequence.
$a_8 = 13 \times 2187 = 28{,}431$	
The eighth term of the given sequence is **28,431**.	

58) Find the sum of the first 10 terms of this sequence: {–4, 16, –64, 256 . . .}

Answer:

$a_1 = -4$	
$n = 10$	Identify the variables given.
$r = \frac{16}{-4} = -4$	
$S_{10} = \frac{-4(1-(-4)^{10})}{1-(-4)}$	
$= \frac{-4(1-1{,}048{,}576)}{5}$	Plug these values into the equation for the partial sum of a geometric sequence.
$= \frac{4{,}194{,}300}{5}$	
$= \mathbf{838{,}860}$	

two

ALGEBRAIC OPERATIONS

lgebra, meaning "restoration" in Arabic, is the mathematical method of finding the unknown. The first algebraic book in Egypt was used to figure out complex inheritances that were to be split among many individuals. Today, algebra is just as necessary when dealing with unknown amounts.

Algebraic Expressions

The foundation of algebra is the **VARIABLE**, an unknown number represented by a symbol (usually a letter such as x or a). Variables can be preceded by a **COEFFICIENT**, which is a constant (i.e., a real number) in front of the variable, such as $4x$ or $-2a$. An **ALGEBRAIC EXPRESSION** is any sum, difference, product, or quotient of variables and numbers (for example $3x^2$, $2x + 7y - 1$, and $\frac{5}{x}$ are algebraic expressions). **TERMS** are any quantities that are added or subtracted (for example, the terms of the expression $x^2 - 3x + 5$ are x^2, $3x$, and 5). A **POLYNOMIAL EXPRESSION** is an algebraic expression where all the exponents on the variables are whole numbers. A polynomial with only two terms is known as a **BINOMIAL**, and one with three terms is a **TRINOMIAL**. A **MONOMIAL** has only one term.

EVALUATING EXPRESSIONS is another way of saying "find the numeric value of an expression if the variable is equal to a certain number." To evaluate the expression, simply plug the given value(s) for the variable(s) into the equation and simplify. Remember to use the order of operations when simplifying:

1. Parentheses
2. Exponents
3. Multiplication
4. Division
5. Addition
6. Subtraction

Simplified expressions are ordered by variable terms alphabetically with highest exponent first then down to constants.

If $m = 4$, find the value of the following expression:
$5(m-2)^3 + 3m^2 - \frac{m}{4} - 1$

Answer:

$5(m-2)^3 + 3m^2 - \frac{m}{4} - 1$	
$= 5(4-2)^3 + 3(4)^2 - \frac{4}{4} - 1$	Plug the value 4 in for m in the expression.
$= 5(2)^3 + 3(4)^2 - \frac{4}{4} - 1$	Calculate all the expressions inside the parentheses.
$= 5(8) + 3(16) - \frac{4}{4} - 1$	Simplify all exponents.
$= 40 + 48 - 1 - 1$	Perform multiplication and division from left to right.
$= \mathbf{86}$	Perform addition and subtraction from left to right.

Operations with Expressions

Adding and Subtracting

Expressions can be added or subtracted by simply adding and subtracting LIKE TERMS, which are terms with the same variable part (the variables must be the same, with the same exponents on each variable). For example, in the expressions $2x + 3xy - 2z$ and $6y + 2xy$, the like terms are $3xy$ and $2xy$. Adding the two expressions yields the new expression $2x + 6xy - 2z + 6y$. Note that the other terms did not change; they cannot be combined because they have different variables.

If $a = 12x + 7xy - 9y$ and $b = 8x - 9xz + 7z$, what is $a + b$?

Answer:

$a + b =$ $(12x + 8x) + 7xy - 9y - 9xz$ $+ 7z =$ **$20x + 7xy - 9y - 9xz + 7z$**	The only like terms in both expressions are $12x$ and $8x$, so these two terms will be added, and all other terms will remain the same.

Operations with polynomials can always be checked by evaluating equivalent expressions for the same value.

Distributing and Factoring

Distributing and factoring can be seen as two sides of the same coin. DISTRIBUTION multiplies each term in the first factor by each term in the second factor to get rid of parentheses. FACTORING reverses this process, taking a polynomial in standard form and writing it as a product of two or more factors.

When distributing a monomial through a polynomial, the expression outside the parentheses is multiplied by each term inside the parentheses. Using the rules of exponents, coefficients are multiplied and exponents are added.

When simplifying two polynomials, each term in the first polynomial must multiply each term in the second polynomial. A binomial (two terms) multiplied by a binomial, will require 2 × 2 or 4 multiplications. For the binomial × binomial case, this process is sometimes called **FOIL**, which stands for first, outside, inside, and last. These terms refer to the placement of each term of the expression: multiply the first term in each expression, then the outside terms, then the inside terms, and finally the last terms. A binomial (two terms) multiplied by a trinomial (three terms), will require 2 × 3 or 6 products to simplify. The first term in the first polynomial multiplies each of the three terms in the second polynomial, then the second term in the first polynomial multiplies each of the three terms in the second polynomial. A trinomial (three terms) by a trinomial will require 3 × 3 or 9 products, and so on.

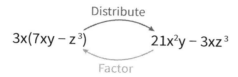

Figure 2.1. Distribution and Factoring

Factoring is the reverse of distributing: the first step is always to remove ("undistribute") the GCF of all the terms, if there is a GCF (besides 1). The GCF is the product of any constants and/or variables that <u>every</u> term shares. (For example, the GCF of $12x^3$, $15x^2$ and $6xy^2$ is $3x$ because $3x$ evenly divides all three terms.) This shared factor can be taken out of each term and moved to the outside of the parentheses, leaving behind a polynomial where each term is the original term divided by the GCF. (The remaining terms for the terms in the example would be $4x^2$, $5x$, and $2xy$.) It may be possible to factor the polynomial in the parentheses further, depending on the problem.

EXAMPLES

1) Expand the following expression: $5x(x^2 - 2c + 10)$

Answer:

$5x(x^2 - 2c + 10)$

$(5x)(x^2) = 5x^3$

$(5x)(-2c) = -10xc$ | Distribute and multiply the term outside the parentheses to all three terms inside the parentheses.

$(5x)(10) = 50x$

$= 5x^3 - 10xc + 50x$

2) Expand the following expression: $(x^2 - 5)(2x - x^3)$

Answer:

$(x^2 - 5)(2x - x^3)$

$(x^2)(2x) = 2x^3$

$(x^2)(-x^3) = -x^5$

$(-5)(2x) = -10x$ Apply FOIL: first, outside, inside, and last.

$(-5)(-x^3) = 5x^3$

$= 2x^3 - x^5 - 10x + 5x^3$ Combine like terms and put them in order.

$= -x^5 + 7x^3 - 10x$

3) Factor the expression $16z^2 + 48z$

Answer:

$16z^2 + 48z$

$= 16z(z + 3)$ Both terms have a z, and 16 is a common factor of both 16 and 48. So the greatest common factor is $16z$. Factor out the GCF.

4) Factor the expression $6m^3 + 12m^3n - 9m^2$

Answer:

$6m^3 + 12m^3n - 9m^2$

$= 3m^2(2m + 4mn - 3)$ All the terms share the factor m^2, and 3 is the greatest common factor of 6, 12, and 9. So, the GCF is $3m^2$.

Factoring Trinomials

If the leading coefficient is $a = 1$, the trinomial is in the form $x^2 + bx + c$ and can often be rewritten in the factored form, as a product of two binomials: $(x + m)(x + n)$. Recall that the product of two binomials can be written in expanded form $x^2 + mx + nx + mn$. Equating this expression with $x^2 + bx + c$, the constant term c would have to equal the product mn. Thus, to work backward from the trinomial to the factored form, consider all the numbers m and n that multiply to make c. For example, to factor $x^2 + 8x + 12$, consider all the pairs that multiply to be 12 ($12 = 1 \times 12$ or 2×6 or 3×4). Choose the pair that will make the coefficient of the middle term (8) when added. In this example 2 and 6 add to 8, so making $m = 2$ and $n = 6$ in the expanded form gives:

$x^2 + 8x + 12 = x^2 + 2x + 6x + 12$	
$= (x^2 + 2x) + (6x + 12)$	Group the first two terms and the last two terms.
$= x(x + 6) + 2(x + 6)$	Factor the GCF out of each set of parentheses.

$$= (x + 6)(x + 2)$$

The two terms now have the common factor $(x + 6)$, which can be removed, leaving $(x + 2)$ and the original polynomial is factored.

In general:

$$x^2 + bx + c = x^2 + mx + nx + mn, \text{ where } c = mn \text{ and } b = m + n$$

$= (x^2 + mx) + (nx + mn)$	Group.
$= x(x + m) + n(x + m)$	Factor each group.
$= (x + m)(x + n)$	Factor out the common binomial.

Note that if none of the factors of c add to the value b, then the trinomial cannot be factored, and is called **PRIME**.

If the leading coefficient is not 1 ($a \neq 1$), first make sure that any common factors among the three terms are factored out. If the a-value is negative, factor out –1 first as well. If the a-value of the new polynomial in the parentheses is still not 1, follow this rule: Identify two values r and s that multiply to be ac and add to be b. Then write the polynomial in this form: $ax^2 + bx + c = ax^2 + rx + sx + c$, and proceed by grouping, factoring, and removing the common binomial as above.

There are a few special factoring cases worth memorizing: difference of squares, binomial squared, and the sum and difference of cubes.

- **Difference of squares** (each term is a square and they are subtracted):
  - ❖ $a^2 - b^2 = (a + b)(a - b)$
  - ❖ Note that a SUM of squares is never factorable.
- **Binomial squared**:
  - ❖ $a^2 + 2ab + b^2 = (a + b)(a + b) = (a + b)^2$
- **Sum and difference of cubes**:
  - ❖ $a^3 + b^3 = (a + b)(a^2 - ab + b^2)$
  - ❖ $a^3 - b^3 = (a - b)(a^2 + ab + b^2)$
  - ❖ Note that the second factor in these factorizations will never be able to be factored further.

SAMPLE QUESTIONS

1) Factor: $16x^2 + 52x + 30$

Answer:

$16x^2 + 52x + 30$	
$= 2(8x^2 + 26x + 15)$	Remove the GCF of 2.

$= 2(8x^2 + 6x + 20x + 15)$	To factor the polynomial in the parentheses, calculate $ac = (8)(15) = 120$, and consider all the pairs of numbers that multiply to be 120: $1 \times 120, 2 \times 60, 3 \times 40, 4 \times 30, 5 \times 24, 6 \times 20, 8 \times 15$, and 10×12. Of these pairs, choose the pair that adds to be the b-value 26 (6 and 20).
$= 2[(8x^2 + 6x) + (20x + 15)]$	Group.
$= 2[(2x(4x + 3) + 5(4x + 3)]$	Factor out the GCF of each group.
$= 2[(4x + 3)(2x + 5)]$	Factor out the common binomial.
2(4x + 3)(2x + 5)	

If there are no values r and s that multiply to be ac and add to be b, then the polynomial is prime and cannot be factored.

8) Factor $16x^2 + 52x + 30$

Answer:

$16x^2 + 52x + 30$	
$= 2(8x^2 + 26x + 15)$	Remove the GCF of 2.
$= 2(8x^2 + 6x + 20x + 15)$	Factor the polynomial in the parentheses. Calculate $ac = (8)(15) = 120$. Consider all the pairs of numbers that multiply to be 120: $1 \times 120, 2 \times 60, 3 \times 40, 4 \times 30, 5 \times 24, 6 \times 20, 8 \times 15$, and 10×12. Choose the pair that adds up to the b-value 26 (6 and 20).
$= 2[(8x^2 + 6x) + (20x + 15)]$	Group.
$= 2[(2x(4x + 3) + 5(4x + 3)]$	Factor out the GCF of each group.
$= \mathbf{2(4x + 3)(2x + 5)}$	Factor out the common binomial.

three

EQUATIONS AND INEQUALITIES

Linear Equations

An **EQUATION** states that two expressions are equal to each other. Polynomial equations are categorized by the highest power of the variables they contain: the highest power of any exponent of a linear equation is 1, a quadratic equation has a variable raised to the second power, a cubic equation has a variable raised to the third power, and so on.

Solving Linear Equations

Solving an equation means finding the value or values of the variable that make the equation true. To solve a linear equation, it is necessary to manipulate the terms so that the variable being solved for appears alone on one side of the equal sign while everything else in the equation is on the other side.

The way to solve linear equations is to "undo" all the operations that connect numbers to the variable of interest. Follow these steps:

1. Eliminate fractions by multiplying each side by the least common multiple of any denominators.
2. Distribute to eliminate parentheses, braces, and brackets.
3. Combine like terms.
4. Use addition or subtraction to collect all terms containing the variable of interest to one side, and all terms not containing the variable to the other side.
5. Use multiplication or division to remove coefficients from the variable of interest.

Sometimes there are no numeric values in the equation or there are a mix of numerous variables and constants. The goal is to solve the equation for one of the variables in terms of the other variables. In this

On multiple choice tests, it is often easier to plug the possible values into the equation and determine which solution makes the equation true than to solve the equation.

case, the answer will be an expression involving numbers and letters instead of a numeric value.

EXAMPLES

1) Solve for x: $\dfrac{100(x+5)}{20} = 1$

Answer:

$\dfrac{100(x+5)}{20} = 1$	
$(20)\left(\dfrac{100(x+5)}{20}\right) = (1)(20)$ $100(x+5) = 20$	Multiply both sides by 20 to cancel out the denominator.
$100x + 500 = 20$	Distribute 100 through the parentheses.
$100x = -480$	"Undo" the +500 by subtracting 500 on both sides of the equation to isolate the variable term.
$x = \dfrac{-480}{100}$	"Undo" the multiplication by 100 by dividing by 100 on both sides to solve for x.
$x = \mathbf{-4.8}$	

2) Solve for x: $2(x+2)^2 - 2x^2 + 10 = 42$

Answer:

$2(x+2)^2 - 2x^2 + 10 = 42$	
$2(x+2)(x+2) - 2x^2 + 10 = 42$	Eliminate the exponents on the left side.
$2(x^2 + 4x + 4) - 2x^2 + 10 = 42$	Apply FOIL.
$2x^2 + 8x + 8 - 2x^2 + 10 = 42$	Distribute the 2.
$8x + 18 = 42$	Combine like terms on the left-hand side.
$8x = 24$	Isolate the variable. "Undo" +18 by subtracting 18 on both sides.
$x = \mathbf{3}$	"Undo" multiplication by 8 by dividing both sides by 8.

3) Solve the equation for D: $\dfrac{A(3B+2D)}{2N} = 5M - 6$

Answer:

$\dfrac{A(3B+2D)}{2N} = 5M - 6$	
$3AB + 2AD = 10MN - 12N$	Multiply both sides by 2N to clear the fraction, and distribute the A through the parentheses.

$2AD = 10MN - 12N - 3AB$	Isolate the term with the D in it by moving $3AB$ to the other side of the equation.
$D = \dfrac{(10MN - 12N - 3AB)}{2A}$	Divide both sides by $2A$ to get D alone on the right-hand side.

Graphs of Linear Equations

The most common way to write a linear equation is **SLOPE-INTERCEPT FORM**, $y = mx + b$. In this equation, m is the slope, which describes how steep the line is, and b is the y-intercept. Slope is often described as "rise over run" because it is calculated as the difference in y-values (rise) over the difference in x-values (run). The slope of the line is also the rate of change of the dependent variable y with respect to the independent variable x. The y-intercept is the point where the line crosses the y-axis, or where x equals zero.

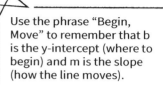

Use the phrase "Begin, Move" to remember that b is the y-intercept (where to begin) and m is the slope (how the line moves).

To graph a linear equation, identify the y-intercept and place that point on the y-axis. If the slope is not written as a fraction, make it a fraction by writing it over 1 $\left(\frac{m}{1}\right)$. Then use the slope to count up (or down, if negative) the "rise" part of the slope and over the "run" part of the slope to find a second point. These points can then be connected to draw the line.

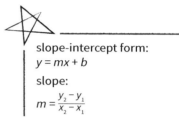

slope-intercept form:
$y = mx + b$
slope:
$m = \dfrac{y_2 - y_1}{x_2 - x_1}$

To find the equation of a line, identify the y-intercept, if possible, on the graph and use two easily identifiable points to find the slope. If the y-intercept is not easily identified, identify the slope by choosing easily identifiable points; then choose one point on the graph, plug the point and the slope values into the equation, and solve for the missing value b.

- standard form: $Ax + By = C$
- $m = -\dfrac{A}{B}$
- x-intercept $= \dfrac{C}{A}$
- y-intercept $= \dfrac{C}{B}$

Another way to express a linear equation is standard form: $Ax + By = C$. In order to graph equations in this form, it is often easiest to convert them to point-slope form. Alternately, it is easy to find the x- or y-intercept from this form, and once these two points are known, a line can be drawn through them. To find the x-intercept, simply make $y = 0$ and solve for x. Similarly, to find the y-intercept, make $x = 0$ and solve for y.

GO ON

EXAMPLES

1) What is the slope of the line whose equation is $6x - 2y - 8 = 0$?

Answer:

$6x - 2y - 8 = 0$	
$-2y = -6x + 8$ $$y = \frac{-6x + 8}{-2}$$ $y = 3x - 4$	Rearrange the equation into slope-intercept form by solving the equation for y.
$m = 3$	The slope is 3, the value attached to x.

2) What is the equation of the following line?

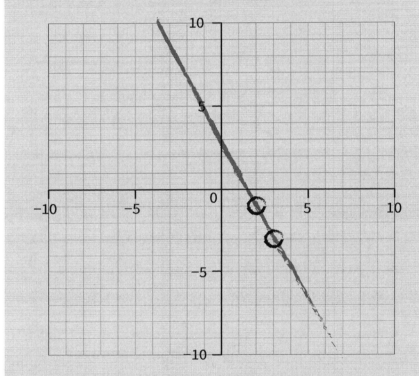

Answer:

$b = 3$	The y-intercept can be identified on the graph as $(0, 3)$.
$$m = \frac{(-3) - (-1)}{3 - 2} = \frac{-2}{1} = -2$$	To find the slope, choose any two points and plug the values into the slope equation. The two points chosen here are $(2, -1)$ and $(3, -3)$.
$y = -2x + 3$	Replace m with -2 and b with 3 in $y = mx + b$.

3) Write the equation of the line which passes through the points $(-2, 5)$ and $(-5, 3)$.

Answer:

$(-2, 5)$ and $(-5, 3)$

$m = \dfrac{3 - 5}{(-5) - (-2)}$ $= \dfrac{-2}{-3}$ $= \dfrac{2}{3}$	Calculate the slope.
$5 = \dfrac{2}{3}(-2) + b$ $5 = \dfrac{-4}{3} + b$ $b = \dfrac{19}{3}$	To find b, plug into the equation $y = mx + b$ the slope for m and a set of points for x and y.
$y = \dfrac{2}{3}x + \dfrac{19}{3}$	Replace m and b to find the equation of the line.

4) What is the equation of the following graph?

Answer:

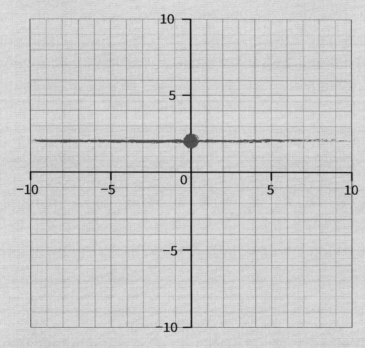

$y = 0x + 2$, **or** $y = 2$

The line has a rise of 0 and a run of 1, so the slope is $\dfrac{0}{1} = 0$. There is no x-intercept. The y-intercept is $(0, 2)$, meaning that the b-value in the slope-intercept form is 2.

Systems of Linear Equations

Systems of equations are sets of equations that include two or more variables. These systems can only be solved when there are at least as many equations as there are variables. Systems involve working with more than one equation to solve for more than one variable. For a system of linear equations, the solution to the system is the set of values for the variables that satisfies every equation in the system. Graphically, this will be the point where every line meets. If the lines are parallel (and hence do not intersect), the system will have no solution. If the lines are multiples of each other, meaning they share all coordinates, then the system has infinitely many solutions (because every point on the line is a solution).

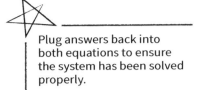

Plug answers back into both equations to ensure the system has been solved properly.

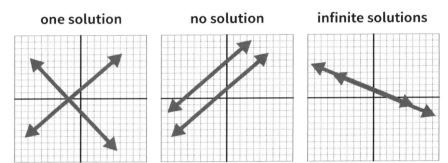

Figure 3.1. Systems of Equations

There are three common methods for solving systems of equations. To perform SUBSTITUTION, solve one equation for one variable, and then plug in the resulting expression for that variable in the second equation. This process works best for systems of two equations with two variables where the coefficient of one or more of the variables is 1.

To solve using ELIMINATION, add or subtract two equations so that one or more variables are eliminated. It's often necessary to multiply one or both of the equations by a scalar (constant) in order to make the variables cancel. Equations can be added or subtracted as many times as necessary to find each variable.

Yet another way to solve a system of linear equations is to use a MATRIX EQUATION. In the matrix equation $AX = B$, A contains the system's coefficients, X contains the variables, and B contains the constants (as shown below). The matrix equation can then be solved by multiplying B by the inverse of A: $X = A^{-1}B$

$$\begin{matrix} ax + by = e \\ cx + dy = f \end{matrix} \rightarrow A = \begin{bmatrix} a & b \\ c & d \end{bmatrix} \quad X = \begin{bmatrix} x \\ y \end{bmatrix} \quad B = \begin{bmatrix} e \\ f \end{bmatrix} \rightarrow AX = B$$

This method can be extended to equations with three or more variables. Technology (such as a graphing calculator) is often employed when solving using this method if more than two variables are involved.

EXAMPLES

1) Solve for x and y:

$2x - 4y = 28$

$4x - 12y = 36$

Answer:

$2x - 4y = 28$ $x = 2y + 14$	Solve the system with substitution. Solve one equation for one variable.
$4x - 12y = 36$ $4(2y + 14) - 12y = 36$ $8y + 56 - 12y = 36$ $-4y = -20$ $y = 5$	Plug in the resulting expression for x in the second equation and simplify.
$2x - 4y = 28$ $2x - 4(5) = 28$ $2x - 20 = 28$ $2x = 48$ $x = 24$ The answer is $y = 5$ and $x = 24$ or **(24, 5)**.	Plug the solved variable into either equation to find the second variable.

2) Solve for the system for x and y:

$3 = -4x + y$

$16x = 4y + 2$

Answer:

$3 = -4x + y$ $y = 4x + 3$	Isolate the variable in one equation.
$16x = 4y + 2$ $16x = 4(4x + 3) + 2$ $16x = 16x + 12 + 2$ $0 = 14$ **No solution exists.**	Plug the expression into the second equation. Both equations have slope 4. This means the graphs of the equations are parallel lines, so no intersection (solution) exists.

3) Solve the system of equations:

$6x + 10y = 18$

$4x + 15y = 37$

Answer:

Because solving for x or y in either equation will result in messy fractions, this problem is best solved using elimination. The goal is to eliminate one of the variables by making the coefficients in front of one set of variables the same, but with different signs, and then adding both equations.

$6x + 10y = 18 \xrightarrow{(-2)} -12x - 20y = -36$ $4x + 15y = 37 \xrightarrow{(3)} 12x + 45y = \underline{111}$	To eliminate the x's in this problem, find the least common multiple of coefficients 6 and 4. The smallest number that both 6 and 4 divide into evenly is 12. Multiply the top equation by -2, and the bottom equation by 3.
$25y = 75$	Add the two equations to eliminate the x's.
$y = 3$	Solve for y.
$6x + 10(3) = 18$ $6x + 30 = 18$ $x = -2$	Replace y with 3 in either of the original equations.
The solution is **(−2, 3).**	

4) Solve the following systems of equations using matrix arithmetic:

$2x - 3y = -5$

$3x - 4y = -8$

Answer:

$\begin{bmatrix} 2 & -3 \\ 3 & -4 \end{bmatrix} \begin{bmatrix} x \\ y \end{bmatrix} = \begin{bmatrix} -5 \\ -8 \end{bmatrix}$	Write the system in matrix form, $AX = B$.
$\begin{bmatrix} 2 & -3 \\ 3 & -4 \end{bmatrix}^{-1}$ $= \frac{1}{(2)(-4)-(-3)(3)} \begin{bmatrix} -4 & 3 \\ -3 & 2 \end{bmatrix} =$ $\begin{bmatrix} -4 & 3 \\ -3 & 2 \end{bmatrix}$	Calculate the inverse of Matrix A.
$\begin{bmatrix} x \\ y \end{bmatrix} = \begin{bmatrix} -4 & 3 \\ -3 & 2 \end{bmatrix} \begin{bmatrix} -5 \\ -8 \end{bmatrix} = \begin{bmatrix} -4 \\ -1 \end{bmatrix}$	Multiply B by the inverse of A.
$x = -4$ $y = -1$	Match up the 2×1 matrices to identify x and y.

Building Equations

In word problems, it is often necessary to translate a verbal description of a relationship into a mathematical equation. No matter the problem, this process can be done using the same steps:

Use the acronym STAR to remember word-problem strategies: Search the problem, Translate into an expression or equation, Answer, and Review.

1. Read the problem carefully and identify what value needs to be solved for.
2. Identify the known and unknown quantities in the problem, and assign the unknown quantities a variable.
3. Create equations using the variables and known quantities.
4. Solve the equations.
5. Check the solution: Does it answer the question asked in the problem? Does it make sense?

EXAMPLES

1) A school is holding a raffle to raise money. There is a $3 entry fee, and each ticket costs $5. If a student paid $28, how many tickets did he buy?

Answer:

Number of tickets = x Cost per ticket = 5 Cost for x tickets = $5x$ Total cost = 28 Entry fee = 3	Identify the quantities.
$5x + 3 = 28$	Set up equations. The total cost for x tickets will be equal to the cost for x tickets plus the $3 flat fee.
$5x + 3 = 28$ $5x = 25$ $x = 5$ The student bought **5 tickets**.	Solve the equation for x.

2) Kelly is selling shirts for her school swim team. There are two prices: a student price and a nonstudent price. During the first week of the sale, Kelly raised $84 by selling 10 shirts to students and 4 shirts to nonstudents. She earned $185 in the second week by selling 20 shirts to students and 10 shirts to nonstudents. What is the student price for a shirt?

Answer:

Student price = s Nonstudent price = n	Assign variables.

$10s + 4n = 84$ $20s + 10n = 185$	Create two equations using the number of shirts Kelly sold and the money she earned.
$10s + 4n = 84$ $10n = -20s + 185$ $n = -2s + 18.5$ $10s + 4(-2s + 18.5) = 84$ $10s - 8s + 74 = 84$ $2s + 74 = 84$ $2s = 10$ $s = 5$	Solve the system of equations using substitution.
The student cost for shirts is **$5**.	

Linear Inequalities

Solving Linear Inequalities

An inequality shows the relationship between two expressions, much like an equation. However, the equal sign is replaced with an inequality symbol that expresses the following relationships:

- ◆ < less than
- ◆ ≤ less than or equal to
- ◆ > greater than
- ◆ ≥ greater than or equal to

Inequalities are read from left to right. For example, the inequality $x \leq 8$ would be read as "x is less than or equal to 8," meaning x has a value smaller than or equal to 8. The set of solutions of an inequality can be expressed using a number line. The shaded region on the number line represents the set of all the numbers that make an inequality true. One major difference between equations and inequalities is that equations generally have a finite number of solutions, while inequalities generally have infinitely many solutions (an entire interval on the number line containing infinitely many values).

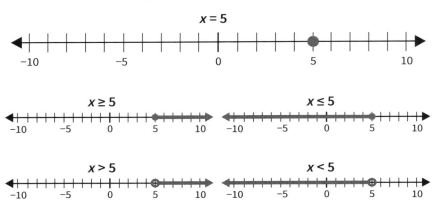

Figure 3.2. Inequalities on a Number Line

Linear inequalities can be solved in the same way as linear equations, with one exception. When multiplying or dividing both sides of an inequality by a negative number, the direction of the inequality sign must reverse—"greater than" becomes "less than" and "less than" becomes "greater than."

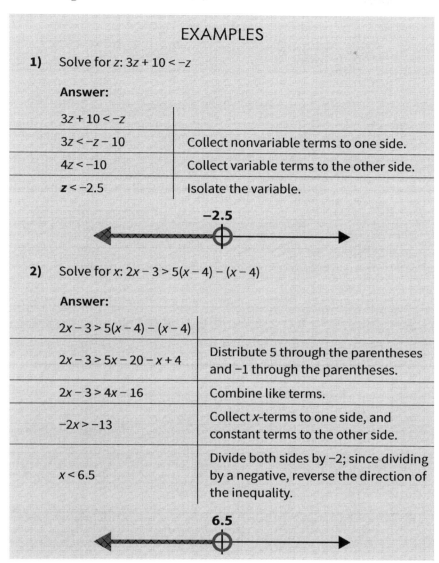

EXAMPLES

1) Solve for z: $3z + 10 < -z$

Answer:

$3z + 10 < -z$	
$3z < -z - 10$	Collect nonvariable terms to one side.
$4z < -10$	Collect variable terms to the other side.
$z < -2.5$	Isolate the variable.

2) Solve for x: $2x - 3 > 5(x - 4) - (x - 4)$

Answer:

$2x - 3 > 5(x - 4) - (x - 4)$	
$2x - 3 > 5x - 20 - x + 4$	Distribute 5 through the parentheses and −1 through the parentheses.
$2x - 3 > 4x - 16$	Combine like terms.
$-2x > -13$	Collect x-terms to one side, and constant terms to the other side.
$x < 6.5$	Divide both sides by −2; since dividing by a negative, reverse the direction of the inequality.

Compound Inequalities

Compound inequalities have more than one inequality expression. Solutions of compound inequalities are the sets of all numbers that make *all* the inequalities true. Some compound inequalities may not have any solutions, some will have solutions that contain some part of the number line, and some will have solutions that include the entire number line.

Table 3.1. Unions and Intersections

Inequality	Meaning in Words	Number Line
$a < x < b$	All values x that are greater than a and less than b	
$a \le x \le b$	All values x that are greater than or equal to a and less than or equal to b	
$x < a \ or \ x > b$	All values of x that are less than a or greater than b	
$x \le a \ or \ x \ge b$	All values of x that are less than or equal to a or greater than or equal to b	

Compound inequalities can be written, solved, and graphed as two separate inequalities. For compound inequalities in which the word *and* is used, the solution to the compound inequality will be the set of numbers on the number line where both inequalities have solutions (where both are shaded). For compound inequalities where *or* is used, the solution to the compound inequality will be *all* the shaded regions for *either* inequality.

EXAMPLES

1) Solve the compound inequalities: $2x + 4 < -18 \ or \ 4(x + 2) > 18$

Answer:

$2x + 4 < -10 \ or \ 4(x + 2) > 18$

$2x < -14$	$4x + 8 > 18$
$x < -7$	$4x > 10$
	$x > 2.5$

Solve each inequality independently.

The solution to the original compound inequality is **the set of all x for which $x < -7$ or $x > 2.5$.**

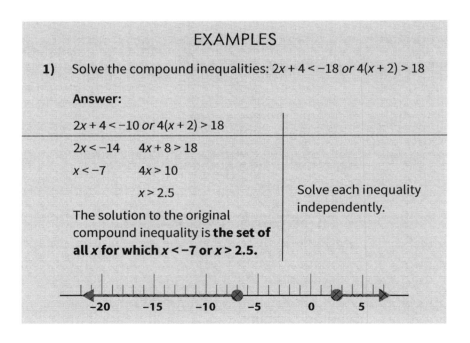

2) Solve the inequality: $-1 \le 3(x+2) - 1 \le x + 3$

Answer:

$-1 \le 3(x+2) - 1 \le x + 3$	
$-1 \le 3(x+2) - 1$ *and* $3(x+2) - 1 \le x + 3$	Break up the compound inequality into two inequalities.
$\begin{aligned}-1 &\le 3x + 6 - 1 \\ -6 &\le 3x \\ -2 &\le x \end{aligned}$ $\begin{aligned}3x + 6 - 1 &\le x + 3 \\ 2x &\le -2 \\ \text{and} \quad x &\le -1 \end{aligned}$	Solve separately.
$-2 \le x \le -1$	The only values of x that satisfy *both* inequalities are the values between -2 and -1 (inclusive).

Graphing Linear Inequalities in Two Variables

Linear inequalities in two variables can be graphed in much the same way as linear equations. Start by graphing the corresponding equation of a line (temporarily replace the inequality with an equal sign, and then graph). This line creates a boundary line of two half-planes. If the inequality is a "greater/less than," the boundary should not be included and a dotted line is used. A solid line is used to indicate that the boundary should be included in the solution when the inequality is "greater/less than or equal to."

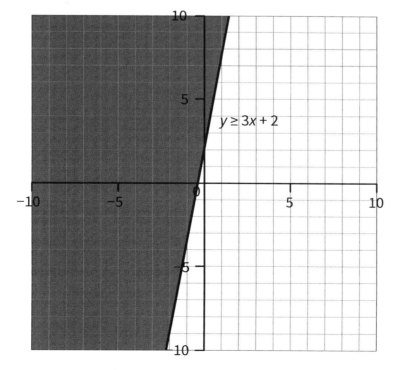

Figure 3.3. Graphing Inequalities

One side of the boundary is the set of all points (x, y) that make the inequality true. This side is shaded to indicate that all these values are solutions. If y is greater than the expression containing x, shade above the line; if it is less than, shade below. A point can also be used to check which side of the line to shade.

A set of two or more linear inequalities is a SYSTEM OF INEQUAL-ITIES. Solutions to the system are all the values of the variables that make every inequality in the system true. Systems of inequalities are solved graphically by graphing all the inequalities in the same plane. The region where all the shaded solutions overlap is the solution to the system.

EXAMPLES

1)   What is the inequality represented on the graph below?

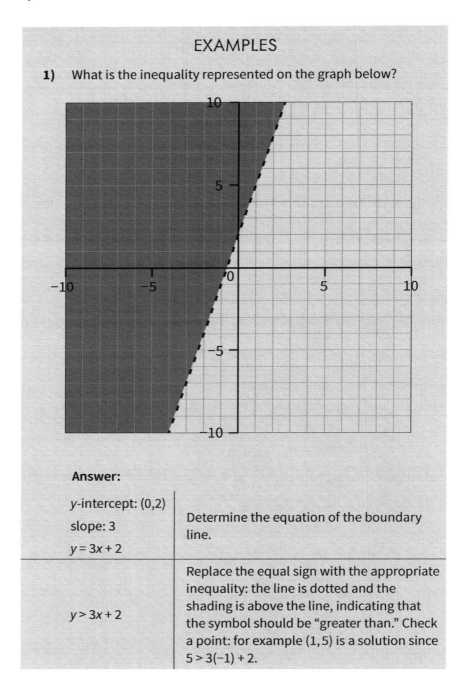

Answer:

y-intercept: $(0,2)$ slope: 3 $y = 3x + 2$	Determine the equation of the boundary line.
$y > 3x + 2$	Replace the equal sign with the appropriate inequality: the line is dotted and the shading is above the line, indicating that the symbol should be "greater than." Check a point: for example $(1, 5)$ is a solution since $5 > 3(-1) + 2$.

2) Graph the following inequality: $3x + 6y \leq 12$.

Answer:

$3x + 6y \leq 12$

$3(0) + 6y = 12$

$y = 2$

y-intercept: $(0, 2)$

$3x + 6(0) \leq 12$

$x = 4$

x-intercept: $(4, 0)$

Find the x- and y-intercepts.

Graph the line using the intercepts, and shade below the line.

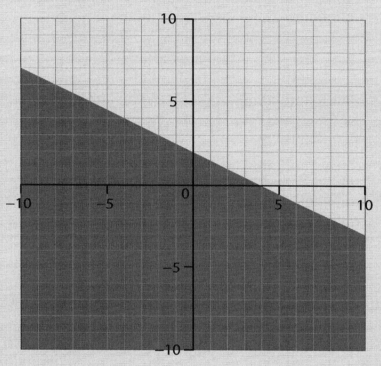

3) Graph the system of inequalities: $-x + y \leq 1, x \geq -1, y > 2x - 4$

Answer:

To solve the system, graph all three inequalities in the same plane; then identify the area where the three solutions overlap. All points (x, y) in this area will be solutions to the system since they satisfy all three inequalities.

GO ON

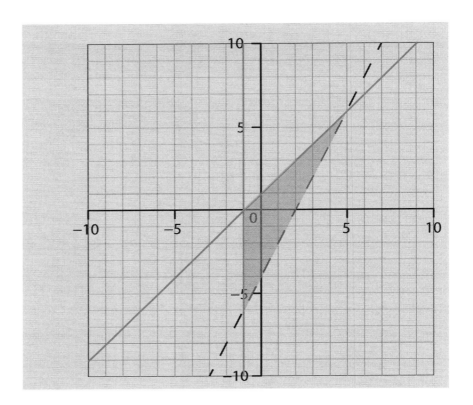

Quadratic Equations and Inequalities

Quadratic equations are degree 2 polynomials; the highest power on the dependent variable is two. While linear functions are represented graphically as lines, the graph of a quadratic function is a **PARABOLA**. The graph of a parabola has three important components. The **VERTEX** is where the graph changes direction. In the parent graph $y = x^2$, the origin $(0,0)$ is the vertex. The **AXIS OF SYMMETRY** is the vertical line that cuts the graph into two equal halves. The line of symmetry always passes through the vertex. On the parent graph, the y-axis is the axis of symmetry. The **ZEROS** or **ROOTS** of the quadratic are the x-intercepts of the graph.

Forms of Quadratic Equations

Quadratic equations can be expressed in two forms:

- **STANDARD FORM: $y = ax^2 + bx + c$**

  Axis of symmetry: $x = -\frac{b}{2a}$ Vertex: $(-\frac{b}{2a}, f(-\frac{b}{2a}))$

- **VERTEX FORM: $y = a(x - h)^2 + k$**

  Vertex: (h, k) Axis of symmetry: $x = h$

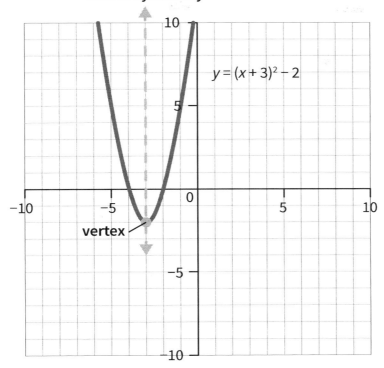

Figure 3.4. Parabola

In both equations, the sign of *a* determines which direction the parabola opens: if *a* is positive, then it opens upward; if *a* is negative, then it opens downward. The wideness or narrowness is also determined by *a*. If the absolute value of *a* is less than one (a proper fraction), then the parabola will get wider the closer $|a|$ is to zero. If the absolute value of *a* is greater than one, then the larger $|a|$ becomes, the narrower the parabola will be.

Equations in vertex form can be converted to standard form by squaring out the $(x - h)^2$ part (using FOIL), distributing the *a*, adding *k*, and simplifying the result.

Equations can be converted from standard form to vertex form by **COMPLETING THE SQUARE**. Take an equation in standard form, $y = ax^2 + bc + c$.

1. Move *c* to the left side of the equation.
2. Divide the entire equation through by *a* (to make the coefficient of x^2 be 1).
3. Take half of the coefficient of *x*, square that number, and then add the result to both sides of the equation.
4. Convert the right side of the equation to a perfect binomial squared, $(x + m)^2$.
5. Isolate *y* to put the equation in proper vertex form.

EXAMPLES

1) What is the line of symmetry for $y = -2(x + 3)^2 + 2$?

Answer:

This quadratic is given in vertex form, with $h = -3$ and $k = 2$. The vertex of this equation is $(-3, 2)$. The line of symmetry is the vertical line that passes through this point. Since the x-value of the point is -3, the line of symmetry is $x = -3$.

2) What is the vertex of the parabola $y = -3x^2 + 24x - 27$?

Answer:

$y = -3x^2 + 24x - 27$	
$x = -\dfrac{b}{2a}$ where $a = -3, b = 24$ $x = -\dfrac{24}{2(-3)} = 4$	This quadratic equation is in standard form. Use the formula for finding the x-value of the vertex.
$y = -3(4)^2 + 24(4) - 27 = 21$ The vertex is at $(4, 21)$.	Plug $x = 4$ into the original equation to find the corresponding y-value.

3) Write $y = -3x^2 + 24x - 27$ in vertex form by completing the square.

Answer:

$y = -3x^2 + 24x - 27$	
$y + 27 = -3x^2 + 24x$	Move c to the other side of the equation.
$\dfrac{y}{-3} - 9 = x^2 - 8x$	Divide through by a (-3 in this example).
$\dfrac{y}{-3} - 9 + 16 = x^2 - 8x$ $+ 16$	Take half of the new b, square it, and add that quantity to both sides: $\frac{1}{2}(-8) = -4$. Squaring it gives $(-4)^2 = 16$.
$\dfrac{y}{-3} + 7 = (x - 4)^2$	Simplify the left side, and write the right side as a binomial squared.
$y = -3(x - 4)^2 + 21$	Subtract 7, and then multiply through by -3 to isolate y.

Solving Quadratic Equations

Solving the quadratic equation $ax^2 + bx + c = 0$ finds x-intercepts of the parabola (by making $y = 0$). These are also called the ROOTS or ZEROS of the quadratic function. A quadratic equation may have zero, one, or two real solutions. There are several ways of finding the zeros. One way is to factor the quadratic into a product of two binomials, and then use the zero product property. (If $m \times n = 0$, then either $m = 0$ or $n =$

0.) Another way is to complete the square and square root both sides. One way that works every time is to memorize and use the **QUADRATIC FORMULA**:

$$x = \frac{-b \pm \sqrt{b^2 - 4ac}}{2a}$$

The *a*, *b*, and *c* come from the standard form of quadratic equations above. (Note that to use the quadratic equation, the right-hand side of the equation must be equal to zero.)

The part of the formula under the square root radical ($b^2 - 4ac$) is known as the **DISCRIMINANT**. The discriminant tells how many and what type of roots will result without actually calculating the roots.

With all graphing problems, putting the function into the $y =$ window of a graphing calculator will aid the process of elimination when graphs are examined and compared to answer choices with a focus on properties like axis of symmetry, vertices, and roots of formulas.

Table 3.2. Discriminants

IF $B^2 - 4AC$ IS	THERE WILL BE	AND THE PARABOLA
zero	only 1 real root	has its vertex on the *x*-axis
positive	2 real roots	has **two** *x*-intercepts
negative	0 real roots 2 complex roots	has **no** *x*-intercepts

EXAMPLES

1) Find the zeros of the quadratic equation: $y = -(x + 3)^2 + 1$.

Answer:

Method 1: Make $y = 0$; isolate x by square rooting both sides:

$0 = -(x + 3)^2 + 1$	Make $y = 0$.
$-1 = -(x + 3)^2$	Subtract 1 from both sides.
$1 = (x + 3)^2$	Divide by -1 on both sides.
$(x + 3) = \pm 1$	Square root both sides. Don't forget to write plus OR minus 1.
$(x + 3) = 1$ *or* $(x + 3) = -1$	Write two equations using +1 and -1.
$x = -2$ *or* $x = -4$	Solve both equations. These are the zeros.

Method 2: Convert vertex form to standard form, and then use the quadratic formula.

$y = -(x + 3)^2 + 1$ $y = -(x^2 + 6x + 9) + 1$ $y = -x^2 - 6x - 8$	Put the equation in standard form by distributing and combining like terms.

$$x = \frac{-b \pm \sqrt{(b^2 - 4ac)}}{2a}$$

$$x = \frac{-(-6) \pm \sqrt{(-6)^2 - 4(-1)(-8)}}{2(-1)}$$

$$x = \frac{6 \pm \sqrt{36 - 32}}{-2}$$

$$x = \frac{6 \pm \sqrt{4}}{-2}$$

$$x = -4, -2$$

Find the zeros using the quadratic formula.

2) Find the root(s) for: $z^2 - 4z + 4 = 0$

Answer:

This polynomial can be factored in the form $(z - 2)(z - 2) = 0$, so the only root is $z = 2$. There is only one x-intercept, and the vertex of the graph is *on* the x-axis.

3) Write a quadratic function that has zeros at $x = -3$ and $x = 2$ that passes through the point $(-2, 8)$.

Answer:

If the quadratic has zeros at $x = -3$ and $x = 2$, then it has factors of $(x + 3)$ and $(x - 2)$. The quadratic function can be written in the factored form $y = a(x + 3)(x - 2)$. To find the a-value, plug in the point $(-2, 8)$ for x and y:

$$8 = a(-2 + 3)(-2 - 2)$$

$$8 = a(-4)$$

$$a = -2$$

The quadratic function is $y = -2(x + 3)(x - 2)$.

Graphing Quadratic Equations

The final expected quadratic skills are graphing a quadratic function given its equation and determining the equation of a quadratic function from its graph. The equation's form determines which quantities are easiest to obtain:

Table 3.3 Obtaining Quantities from Quadratic Functions

Name of Form	Equation of Quadratic	Easiest Quantity to Find	How to Find Other Quantities
vertex form	$y = a(x - h)^2 + k$	vertex at (h, k) and axis of symmetry $x = h$	Find zeros by making $y = 0$ and solving for x.
factored form	$y = a(x - m)(x - n)$	x-intercepts at $x = m$ and $x = n$	Find axis of symmetry by averaging m and n: $x = \frac{m + n}{2}$. This is also the x-value of the vertex.

Name of Form	Equation of Quadratic	Easiest Quantity to Find	How to Find Other Quantities
standard form	$y = ax^2 + bx + c$	y – intercept at $(0, c)$	Find axis of symmetry and x-value of the vertex using $x = \frac{-b}{2a}$. Find zeros using quadratic formula.

To graph a quadratic function, first determine if the graph opens up or down by examining the a-value. Then determine the quantity that is easiest to find based on the form given, and find the vertex. Then other values can be found, if necessary, by choosing x-values and finding the corresponding y-values. Using symmetry instantly doubles the number of points that are known.

Given the graph of a parabola, the easiest way to write a quadratic equation is to identify the vertex and insert the h- and k-values into the vertex form of the equation. The a-value can be determined by finding another point the graph goes through, plugging these values in for x and y, and solving for a.

EXAMPLES

1) Graph the quadratic $y = 2(x - 3)^2 + 4$.

Answer:

Start by marking the vertex at $(3, 4)$ and recognizing this parabola opens upward. The line of symmetry is $x = 3$. Now, plug in an easy value for x to get one point on the curve; then use symmetry to find another point. In this case, choose $x = 2$ (one unit to the left of the line of symmetry) and solve for y:

$y = 2(2 - 3)^2 + 4$

$y = 2(1) + 4$

$y = 6$

GO ON

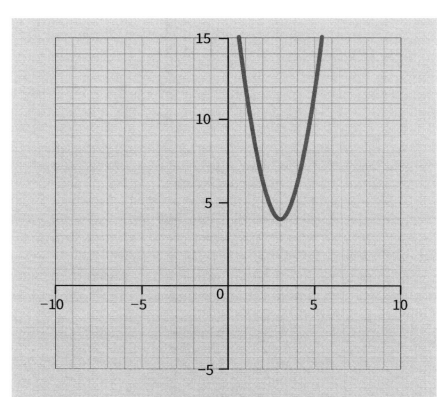

Thus the point (2, 6) is on the curve. Then use symmetry to find the corresponding point one unit to the right of the line of symmetry, which must also have a y value of 6. This point is (4, 6). Draw a parabola through the points.

2) What is the vertex form of the equation shown on the following graph?

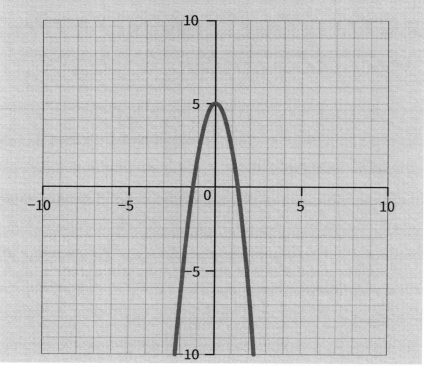

Answer:

$(h, k) = (0, 5)$ $y = a(x - h)^2 + k$ $y = a(x - 0)^2 + 5$ $y = ax^2 + 5$	Locate the vertex and plug values for h and k into the vertex form of the quadratic equation.
$(x, y) = (1, 2)$ $y = ax^2 + 5$ $2 = a(1)^2 + 5$ $a = -3$	Choose another point on the graph to plug into this equation to solve for a.
$y = -3x^2 + 5$	Plug a into the vertex form of the equation.

Quadratic Inequalities

Quadratic inequalities with two variables, such as $y < (x + 3)^2 - 2$ can be graphed much like linear inequalities: graph the equation by treating the inequality symbol as an equal sign, then shade the graph. When y is greater than, shade inside the parabola; when y is less than, shade outside.

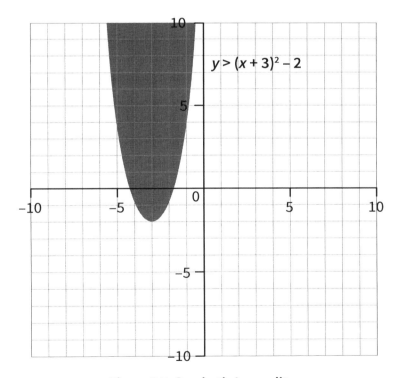

$y > (x + 3)^2 - 2$

Figure 3.5. Quadratic Inequality

Quadratic inequalities with only one variable, such as $x^2 - 4x > 12$, can be solved by first manipulating the inequality so that one side is zero. The zeros can then be found and used to determine where the inequality is greater than zero (positive) or less than zero (negative). Often it helps to set up intervals on a number line and test a value within each range created by the zeros to identify the values that create positive or negative values.

EXAMPLE

Find the values of x such that $x^2 - 4x > 12$.

Answer:

$x^2 - 4x = 12$ $x^2 - 4x - 12 = 0$ $(x + 2)(x - 6) = 0$ $x = -2, 6$	Find the zeros of the inequality.

x	$(x + 2)(x - 6)$	Create a table or number line with the intervals created by the zeros. Use a test value to determine whether the expression is positive or negative.
$-\infty < x < -2$	$+$	
$-2 < x < 6$	$-$	
$6 < x < \infty$	$+$	

$x < -2$ or $x > 6$	Identify the values of x which make the expression positive.

Absolute Value Equations and Inequalities

The **ABSOLUTE VALUE** of a number means the distance between that number and zero. The absolute value of any number is positive since distance is always positive. The notation for absolute value of a number is two vertical bars:

$|-27| = 27$ The distance from -27 to 0 is 27.

$|27| = 27$ The distance from 27 to 0 is 27.

Solving equations and simplifying inequalities with absolute values usually requires writing two equations or inequalities, which are then solved separately using the usual methods of solving equations. To write the two equations, set one equation equal to the positive value of the expression inside the absolute value and the other equal to the negative value. Two inequalities can be written in the same manner. However, the inequality symbol should be flipped for the negative value.

The formal definition of the absolute value is

$$|x| = \begin{cases} -x, & x < 0 \\ x, & x \geq 0 \end{cases}$$

This is true because whenever x is negative, the opposite of x is the answer (for example, $|-5| = -(-5) = 5$, but when x is positive, the answer is just *x*. This type of function is called a PIECE-WISE FUNCTION. It is defined in two (or more) distinct pieces. To graph the absolute value function, graph each piece separately. When $x < 0$ (that is, when it is negative), graph the line $y = -x$. When $x > 0$ (that is, when *x* is positive), graph the line $y = x$. This creates a V-shaped graph that is the parent function for absolute value functions.

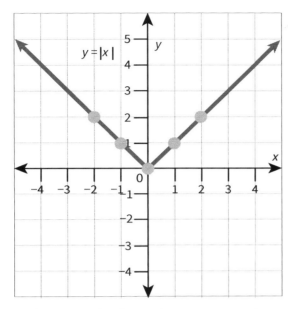

Figure 3.6. Absolute Value Parent Function

EXAMPLES

1) Solve for *x*: $|x - 3| = 27$

Answer:

Set the quantity inside the parentheses equal to 27 or –27, and solve:

$x - 3 = 27$	$x - 3 = -27$
$x = 30$	$x = -24$

2) Solve for r: $\frac{|r - 7|}{5} = 27$

Answer:

The first step is to isolate the absolute value part of the equation. Multiplying both sides by 5 gives:

$|r - 7| = 135$

If the quantity in the absolute value bars is 135 or –135, then the absolute value would be 135:

$r - 7 = 135$	$r - 7 = -135$
$r = 142$	$r = -128$

3) Find the solution set for the following inequality: $\left|\frac{3x}{7}\right| \geq 4 - x$.

Answer:

$\left\|\frac{3x}{7}\right\| \geq 4 - x$	
$\frac{\|3x\|}{7} \geq 4 - x$ $\|3x\| \geq 28 - 7x$	Simplify the equation.
$3x \geq 28 - 7x$ $10x \geq 28$ $x \geq \frac{28}{10}$ $-(3x) \leq 28 - 7x$ $-3x \leq 28 - 7x$ $4x \leq 28$ $x \leq 7$	Create and solve two inequalities. When including the negative answer, flip the inequality.
$\frac{28}{10} \leq x \leq 7$	Combine the two answers to find the solution set.

four

FUNCTIONS

Working with Functions

Functions can be thought of as a process: when something is put in, an action (or operation) is performed, and something different comes out. A FUNCTION is a relationship between two quantities (for example x and y) in which, for every value of the independent variable (usually x), there is exactly one value of the dependent variable (usually y). Briefly, each input has *exactly one* output. Graphically this means the graph passes the VERTICAL LINE TEST: anywhere a vertical line is drawn on the graph, the line hits the curve at exactly one point.

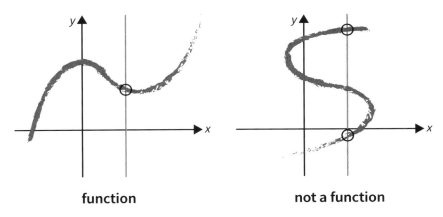

function   **not a function**

Figure 4.1. Vertical Line Test

The notation $f(x)$ or $g(t)$, etc., is often used when a function is being considered. This is FUNCTION NOTATION. The input value is x and the output value y is written as $y = f(x)$. Thus, $f(2)$ represents the output value (or y value) when $x = 2$, and $f(2) = 5$ means that when $x = 2$ is plugged into the $f(x)$ function, the output (y value) is 5. In other words, $f(2) = 5$ represents the point $(2, 5)$ on the graph of $f(x)$.

Every function has an INPUT DOMAIN and OUTPUT RANGE. The domain is the set of all the possible x values that can be used as input values (these are found along the horizontal axis on the graph), and the range includes all the y values or output values that result from applying $f(x)$ (these are found along the vertical axis on the graph). Domain and range are usually intervals of numbers and are often expressed as inequalities, such as $x < 2$ (the domain is all values less than 2) or $3 < x < 15$ (all values between 3 and 15).

Interval notation can also be used to show domain and range. Round brackets indicate that an end value is not included, and square brackets show that it is. The symbol ∪ means *or*, and the symbol ∩ means *and*. For example, the statement (–infinity, 4) ∪ (4, infinity) describes the set of all real numbers except 4.

A function $f(x)$ is EVEN if $f(-x) = f(x)$. Even functions have symmetry across the y-axis. An example of an even function is the parent quadratic $y = x^2$, because any value of x (for example, 3) and its opposite $-x$ (for example, –3) have the same y value (for example, $3^2 = 9$ and $(-3)^2 = 9$). A function is ODD if $f(-x) = -f(x)$. Odd functions have symmetry about the origin. For example, $f(x) = x^3$ is an odd function because $f(3) = 27$, and $f(-3) = -27$. A function may be even, odd, or neither.

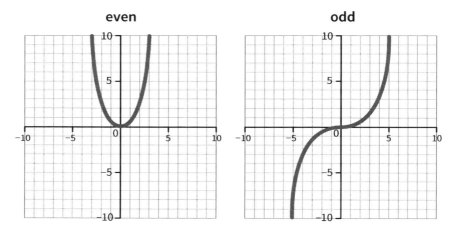

Figure 4.2. Even and Odd Functions

EXAMPLES

1) Evaluate: $f(4)$ if $f(x) = x^3 - 2x + \sqrt{x}$

Answer:

$f(x) = x^3 - 2x + \sqrt{x}$	
$f(4) = (4)^3 - 2(4) + \sqrt{(4)}$	Plug in 4.
$= 64 - 8 + 2$	Follow the PEMDAS order of
$= \mathbf{58}$	operations.

2) What are the domain and range of the following function?

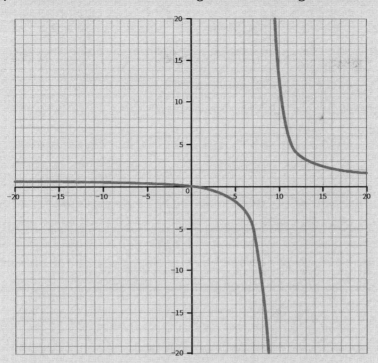

Answer:

This function has an asymptote at $x = 9$, so is not defined there. Otherwise, the function is defined for all other values of x.

D: $-\infty < x < 9$ or $9 < x < \infty$

Since the function has a horizontal asymptote at $y = 1$ that it never crosses, the function never takes the value 1, so the range is all real numbers except 1: **R:** $-\infty < y < 1$ *or* $1 < y < \infty$.

3) Which of the following represents a function?

A.

x	G(x)
0	0
1	1
2	2
1	3

B.

x	F(x)
0	1
0	2
0	3
0	4

C.

T	F(T)
1	1
2	2
3	3
4	4

D.

X	F(X)
0	0
5	1
0	2
5	3

Answer:

Put any function into the $y =$ part of a calculator and look at the table to get domain and range values. Looking at −100, −10, 0, 10, and 100 give a sense about any function's limitations.

For a set of numbers to represent a function, every input must generate a unique output. Therefore, if the same input (x) appears more than once in the table, determine if that input has two different outputs. If so, then the table does not represent a function.

A. This table is not a function because input value 1 has two different outputs (1 and 3).

B. Table B is not function because 0 is the only input and results in four different values.

C. This table shows a function because each input has one output.

D. This table also has one input going to two different values, so it is not a function.

4) What is the domain and the range of the following graph?

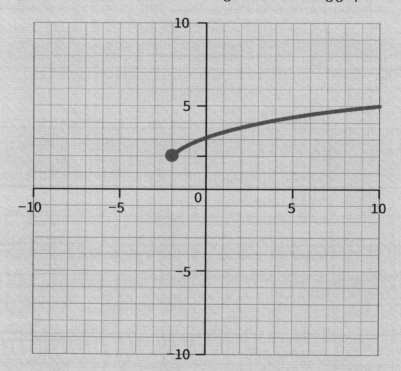

Answer:

For the domain, this graph goes on to the right to positive infinity. Its leftmost point, however, is $x = -2$. Therefore, its domain is all real numbers equal to or greater than −2, **D: − 2 ≤ x < ∞**, or **[−2, ∞)**.

The lowest range value is $y = 2$. Although it has a decreasing slope, this function continues to rise. Therefore, the domain is all real numbers greater than 2, **R: 2 ≤ y < ∞ or [2, ∞)**.

Inverse Functions

INVERSE FUNCTIONS switch the inputs and the outputs of a function. If $f(x) = k$ then the inverse of that function would read $f^{-1}(k) = x$. The domain of $f^{-1}(x)$ is the range of $f(x)$, and the range of $f^{-1}(x)$ is the domain of $f(x)$. If point (a, b) is on the graph of $f(x)$, then point (b, a) will be on the graph of $f^{-1}(x)$. Because of this fact, the graph of $f^{-1}(x)$ is a reflection of the graph of $f(x)$ across the line $y = x$. Inverse functions "undo" all the operations of the original function.

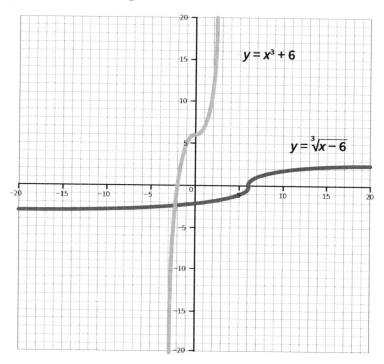

Figure 4.3. Inverse Functions

The steps for finding an inverse function are:

1. Replace $f(x)$ with y to make it easier manipulate the equation.
2. Switch the x and y.
3. Solve for y.
4. Label the inverse function as $f^{-1}(x) =$.

EXAMPLESS

1) What is the inverse of function of $f(x) = 5x + 5$?

   Answer:

$y = 5x + 5$	Replace $f(x)$ with y
$x = 5y + 5$	Switch the places of y and x.

$$x = 5y + 5$$

$$x - 5 = 5y$$ Solve for y.

$$y = \frac{x}{5} - 1$$

$$\mathbf{f^{-1}(x) = \frac{x}{5} - 1}$$

2) Find the inverse of the graph of $f(x) = -1 - \frac{1}{5}x$

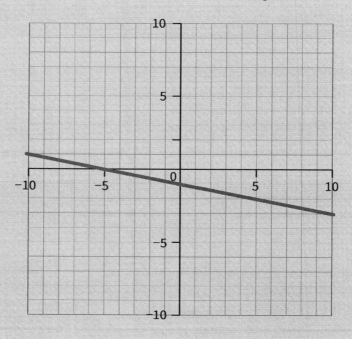

Answer:

This is a linear graph with some clear coordinates: $(-5, 0)$, $(0, -1)$, $(5, -2)$, and $(10, -3)$. This means the inverse function will have coordinate $(0, -5)$, $(-1, 0)$, $(-2, 5)$, and $(-3, 10)$. The inverse function is reflected over the line $y = x$ and is the line $f^{-1}(x) = -5(x + 1)$ below.

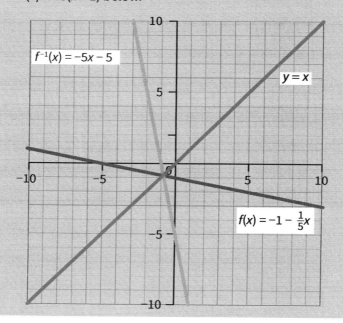

Compound Functions

COMPOUND FUNCTIONS take two or more functions and combine them using operations or composition. Functions can be combined using addition, subtraction, multiplication, or division:

$$\text{addition: } (f + g)(x) = f(x) + g(x)$$

$$\text{subtraction: } (f - g)(x) = f(x) - g(x)$$

$$\text{multiplication: } (fg)(x) = f(x)g(x)$$

$$\text{division: } \left(\frac{f}{g}\right)(x) = \frac{f(x)}{g(x)} \text{ (note that } g(x) \neq 0)$$

Functions can also be combined using **COMPOSITION**. Composition of functions is indicated by the notation $(f \circ g)(x)$. Note that the $\circ$ symbol does NOT mean multiply. It means take the output of $g(x)$ and make it the input of $f(x)$:

$$(f \circ g)(x) = f(g(x))$$

This equation is read f of g of x, and will be a new function of x. Note that order is important. In general, $f(g(x)) \neq g(f(x))$. They *will* be equal when $f(x)$ and $g(x)$ are inverses of each other, however, as both will simplify to the original input x. This is because performing a function on a value and then using that output as the input to the inverse function should bring you back to the original value.

The domain of a composition function is the set of x values that are in the domain of the "inside" function $g(x)$ such that $g(x)$ is in the domain of the outside function $f(x)$. For example, if $f(x) = \frac{1}{x}$ and $g(x) = \sqrt{x}$, $f(g(x))$ has a domain of $x > 0$ because $g(x)$ has a domain of $x \geq 0$. But when $f(x)$ is applied to the $\sqrt{x}$ function, the composition function becomes $\frac{1}{\sqrt{x}}$ and the value $x = 0$ is no longer allowed because it would result in 0 in the denominator, so the domain must be further restricted.

EXAMPLES

1) If $z(x) = 3x - 3$ and $y(x) = 2x - 1$, find $(y \circ z)(-4)$.

Answer:

$(y \circ z)(-4) = y(z(-4))$	
$z(-4)$ $= 3(-4) - 3$ $= -12 - 3$ $= -15$	Starting on the inside, evaluate z.
$y(z(-4))$ $= y(-15)$ $= 2(-15) - 1$ $= -30 - 1$ $= \mathbf{-31}$	Replace $z(-4)$ with -15, and simplify.

2) Find $(k \circ t)(x)$ if $k(x) = \frac{1}{2}x - 3$ and $t(x) = \frac{1}{2}x - 2$.

Answer:

$(k \circ t)(x) = k(t(x))$	
$= k\left(\frac{1}{2}x - 2\right)$	Replace x in the $k(x)$ function with $\left(\frac{1}{2}x - 2\right)$
$= \frac{1}{2}\left(\frac{1}{2}x - 2\right) - 3$	
$= \frac{1}{4}x - 1 - 3$	Simplify.
$= \frac{1}{4}x - 4$	
$(k \circ t)(x) = \frac{1}{4}x - 4$	

3) The wait (W) to get on a ride at an amusement park depends on the number of people (N) in the park. The number of people in the park depends on the number of hours, t, that the park has been open. Suppose $N(t) = 400t$ and $W(N) = 5(1.2)^{\frac{N}{100}}$. What is the value and the meaning in context of $N(4)$ and $W(N(4))$?

Answer:

$N(4) = 400(4) = 1600$ and means that 4 hours after the park opens there are 1600 people in the park. $W(N(4)) = W(1600) = 96$ and means that 4 hours after the park opens the wait time is about **96 minutes** for the ride.

Transforming Functions

Many functions can be graphed using simple transformation of parent functions. Transformations include reflections across axes, vertical and horizontal translations (or shifts), and vertical or horizontal stretches or compressions. The table gives the effect of each transformation to the graph of any function $y = f(x)$.

Table 4.1. Effects of Transformations

EQUATION	EFFECT ON GRAPH
$y = -f(x)$	reflection across the x-axis (vertical reflection)
$y = f(x) + k$	vertical shift up k units ($k > 0$) or down k units ($k < 0$)
$y = kf(x)$	vertical stretch (if $k > 1$) or compression (if $k < 1$)
$y = f(-x)$	reflection across the y-axis (horizontal reflection)
$y = f(x + k)$	horizontal shift right k units ($k < 0$) or left k units ($k > 0$)
$y = f(kx)$	horizontal stretch ($k < 1$) or compression ($k > 1$)

Note that the first three equations have an operation applied to the *outside* of the function $f(x)$ and these all cause *vertical changes* to the graph of the function that are *intuitive* (for example, adding a value moves it up). The last three equations have an operation applied to the *inside* of the function $f(x)$ and these all cause *horizontal changes* to the graph of the function that are *counterintuitive* (for example, multiplying the x's by a fraction results in stretch, not compression, which would seem more intuitive). It is helpful to group these patterns together to remember how each transformation affects the graph.

EXAMPLES

1) Graph: $y = |x + 1| + 4$

Answer:

This function is the absolute value function with a vertical shift up of 4 units (since the 4 is outside the absolute value bars), and a horizontal shift left of 1 unit (since it is inside the bars). The vertex of the graph is at $(-1, 4)$ and the line $x = -1$ is an axis of symmetry.

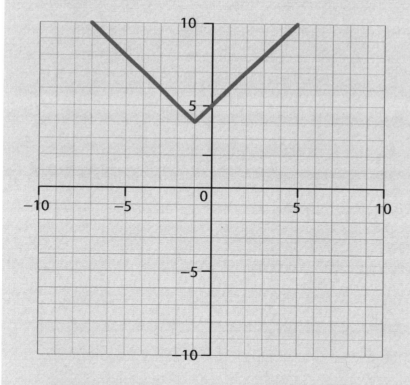

2) Graph: $y = -3|x - 2| + 2$

Answer:

The negative sign in front of the absolute value means the graph will be reflected across the x-axis, so it will open down. The 3 causes a vertical stretch of the function, which results in a narrower graph. The basic curve is shifted 2 units right (since the

−2 is an inside change) and 2 units up (since the +2 is an outside change), so the vertex is at (2, 2).

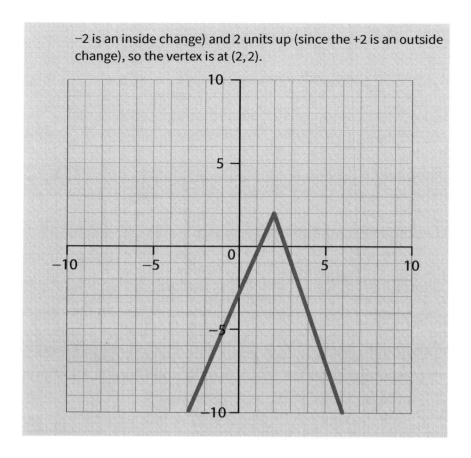

Exponential and Logarithmic Functions

Exponential Functions

An **EXPONENTIAL FUNCTION** has a constant base and a variable in the exponent: $f(x) = b^x$ is an exponential function with base b and exponent x. The value b is the quantity that the y value is multiplied by each time the x value is increased by 1. When looking at a table of values, an exponential function can be identified because the $f(x)$ values are being multiplied. (In contrast, linear $f(x)$ values are being added to.)

The graph of the exponential parent function does not cross the x-axis, which is the function's horizontal asymptote. The y-intercept of the function is at $(0, 1)$.

The general formula for an exponential function, $f(x) = ab^{(x - h)} + k$, allows for transformations to be made to the function. The value h moves the function left or right (moving the y-intercept) while the value k moves the function up or down (moving both the y-intercept and the horizontal asymptote). The value a stretches or compresses the function (moving the y-intercept).

Exponential equations have at least one variable in an exponent position. One way to solve these equations is to make the bases on both side of the equation equivalent, and then equate the exponents. Many

To solve an exponential equation, start by looking for a common base:
$4^{x-2} = \sqrt{8}$
can be rewritten as
$(2^2)^{(x-2)} = (2^3)^{\frac{1}{2}}$
If no common base can be found, logarithms can be used to move the variable out of the exponent position.

exponential equations do not have a solution. Negative numbers often lead to no solutions: for example, $2^x = -8$. The domain of exponential functions is only positive numbers, as seen above, so there is no x value that will result in a negative output.

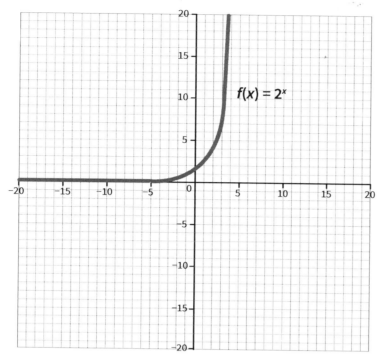

Figure 4.4. Exponential Parent Function

EXAMPLES

1) Graph the exponential function $f(x) = 5^x - 2$.

Answer:

One way to do this is to use a table:

x	$5^x - 2$
−2	$\frac{1}{25} - 2 = -\frac{49}{25}$
−1	$\frac{1}{5} - 2 = -\frac{9}{5}$
0	$1 - 2 = -1$
1	$5 - 2 = 3$
2	$25 - 2 = 23$

GO ON

Another way to graph this is simply to see this function as the parent function $y = b^x$ (with $b = 5$), shifted down by a vertical shift of 2 units. Thus the new horizontal asymptote will be at $y = 2$, and the new y-intercept will be $y = -1$.

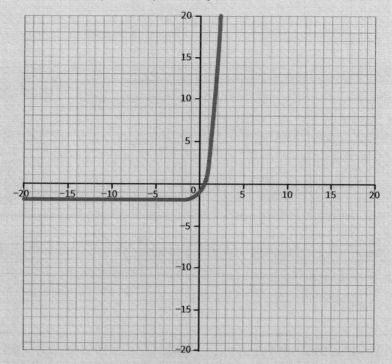

2) If the height of grass in a yard in a humid summer week grows by 5% every day, how much taller would the grass be after six days?

Answer:

Any time a question concerns growth or decay, an exponential function must be created to solve it. In this case, create a table with initial value a, and a daily growth rate of $(1+0.05) = 1.05$ per day.

Days (x)	Height (h)
0	a
1	$1.05a$
2	$1.05(1.05a) = (1.05)^2 a$
3	$(1.05)^2 (1.05a) = (1.05)^3 a$
x	$(1.05)^x a$

After six days the height of the grass is $(1.05)^6 = $ **1.34 times as tall**. The grass would grow 34% in one week. Use 6 days because the table starts at 0, not 1.

3)   Solve for x: $4^{x+1} = \frac{1}{256}$

Answer:

$4^{x+1} = \frac{1}{256}$	
$4^{x+1} = 4^{-4}$	Find a common base and rewrite the equation.
$x + 1 = -4$ $x = -5$	Set the exponents equal and solve for x.

Logarithmic Functions

The LOGARITHMIC FUNCTION (LOG) is the inverse of the exponential function.

$$y = \log_3 x \Rightarrow 3^y = x$$

x	y
$\frac{1}{9}$	-2
$\frac{1}{3}$	-1

$$y = \log_3 x \Rightarrow 3^y = x \text{ (continued)}$$

1	0
3	1
9	2
27	3

A log is used to find out to what power an input is raised to get a desired output. In the table, the base is 3. The log function determines to what power 3 must be raised so that $\frac{1}{9}$ is the result in the table (the answer is –2). As with all inverse functions, these exponential and logarithmic functions are reflections of each other across the line $y = x$.

A NATURAL LOGARITHM (LN) has the number e as its base. Like π, e is an irrational number that is a nonterminating decimal. It is usually shortened to 2.71 when doing calculations. Although the proof of e is beyond the scope of this book, e is to be understood as the upper limit of the range of this rational function: $\left(1 + \frac{1}{n}^n\right)$.

GO ON

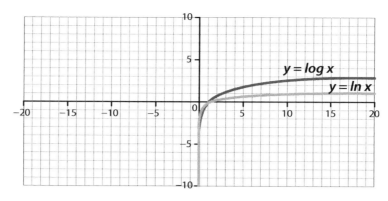

Figure 4.5. Logarithmic Parent Functions

In order to make use of and solve logarithmic functions, log rules are often employed that allow simplification:

Table 4.2. Properties of Logarithms

Change of base	$\log_b(m) = \dfrac{\log(m)}{\log(b)}$
Logs of products	$\log_b(mn) = \log_b(m) + \log_b(n)$
Logs of quotients	$\log_b\left(\dfrac{m}{n}\right) = \log_b(m) - \log_b(n)$
Log of a power	$\log_b(m^n) = n \times \log_b(m)$
Equal logs/equal arguments	$\log_b M = \log_b N \Leftrightarrow M = N$

Note that when the base is not written out, such as in $\log(m)$, it is understood that the base is 10. Just like a 1 is not put in front of a variable because its presence is implicitly understood, 10 is the implicit base whenever a base is not written out.

EXAMPLES

1) Expand $\log_5\left(\dfrac{25}{x}\right)$

Answer:

Since division of a term can be written as a subtraction problem, this simplifies to:

$\log_5(25) - \log_5(x)$

The first term asks "what power of 5 gives 25?" The power is 2. Therefore, the most expanded form is:

$2 - \log_5(x)$

2) Solve for x: $\ln x + \ln 4 = 2\ln 4 - \ln 2$

Answer:

$\ln x + \ln 4 = 2\ln 4 - \ln 2$	
$\ln(4x) = \ln 4^2 - \ln 2$	Apply the log of product and log of exponent rules.
$\ln(4x) = \ln 16 - \ln 2$	

$\ln(4x) = \ln 8$	Follow log of quotient rule.
$4x = 8$ $x = 2$	Set the arguments equal to each other.

3) Solve for x: $2^x = 40$

Answer:

$\log_2 2^x = \log_2 40$	Take the $\log_2$ of both sides.
$x \log_2 2 = \log_2 40$	Drop the x down using properties of logs.
$x = \log_2 40$	$\log_2 2$ simplifies to 1.
$= 5.32$	Use the change of base rule or a calculator to calculate the value of $\log_2(40)$.

Special Equations

There are three exponential function formulas that frequently show up in word problems:

The **Growth Formula:**

$y = a(1 + r)^t$ Initial amount a increases at a rate of r per time period

The **Decay Formula:**

$y = a(1 - r)^t$ Initial amount a decreases at a rate of r per time period

In these formulas, a is the initial amount (at time $t = 0$), r is the rate of growth or decay (written as a decimal in the formula), and t is the number of growth or decay cycles that have passed.

A special case of the growth function is known as the **Compound-Interest Formula**:

$$A = P\left(1 + \frac{r}{n}\right)^{nt}$$

In this formula, A is the future value of an investment, P is the initial deposit (or principal), r is the interest rate as a percentage, n is the number of times interest is compounded within a time period, or how often interest is applied to the account in a year (once per year, $n = 1$; monthly, $n = 12$; etc.), and t is the number of compounding cycles (usually years).

EXAMPLES

1) In the year 2000, the number of text messages sent in a small town totaled 124. If the number of text messages grew every year afterward by 124%, how many years would it take for the number of text messages to surpass 36,000?

Answer:

This is a growth problem that will require using the growth equation:

$y = a(1 + r)^t$.

$y = 124(1 + 1.24)^t$ Write 124% as the decimal 1.24; the initial value is $a = 124$.

$y = 124(2.24)^t$

The question is asking when is $124(2.24)^x > 36,000$. One way to solve this is to graph $y_1 = 124(2.24)^x$ and $y_2 = 36,000$ on a calculator and look for when the first curve exceeds the second curve. Find the intersection of these curves using the features of the calculator. This will give the exact time when the text messages exceed 36,000. This inequality can also be solved by solving the corresponding equations using logarithms, etc. However, it is rarely necessary to do this on a multiple-choice test. Often, the best approach is simply to plug the answer choices into the above equation to find which one works.

2) The half-life of a certain isotope is 5.5 years. If there were 20 grams of one such isotope left after 22 years, what was its original weight?

Answer:

$t = \frac{22}{5.5} = 4$	
$r = 0.5$	Identify the variables.
$a = ?$	
$20 = a(1 - 0.50)^4$	
$20 = a(0.5)^4$	
$20 = a(\frac{1}{2})^4$	
$20 = a(\frac{1}{16})$	Plug these values into the decay formula and solve.
$320 = a$	
The original weight is **320 grams**.	

3) If there were a glitch at a bank and a savings account accrued 5% interest five times per week, what would be the amount earned on a $50 deposit after twelve weeks?

Answer:

$r = 0.05$	
$n = 5$	Identify the variables.
$t = 12$	
$P = 50$	
$A = 50\left(1 + \frac{0.05}{5}\right)^{5(12)}$	Use the compound-interest formula, since this problem has many steps of growth within a time period.
$A = 50(1.01)^{60}$	
$A = 50(1.82) = 90.83$	

90.83 − 50 = $40.83	Subtract the original deposit to find the amount of interest earned.

Polynomial Functions

A polynomial is any equation or expression with two or more terms with whole number exponents. All polynomials with only one variable are functions. The zeros, or roots, of a polynomial function are where the function equals zero and crosses the x-axis.

A linear function is a degree 1 polynomial and always has one zero. A quadratic function is a degree 2 polynomial and always has exactly two roots (including complex roots and counting repeated roots separately). This pattern is extended in the FUNDAMENTAL THEOREM OF ALGEBRA:

A polynomial function with degree $n > 0$ such as $f(x) = ax^n + bx^{n-1} + cx^{n-2} + \ldots + k$, has exactly n (real or complex) roots (some roots may be repeated). Simply stated, whatever the degree of the polynomial is, that is how many roots it will have.

Table 4.3. Zeros of Polynomial Functions

POLYNOMIAL DEGREE, N	NUMBER AND POSSIBLE TYPES OF ZEROS
1	1 real zero (guaranteed)
2	0, 1, or 2 real zeros possible 2 real **or** complex zeros (guaranteed)
3	1, 2, or 3 real zeros possible (there must be at least one real zero) Or 1 real zero (guaranteed) and 2 complex zeros (guaranteed)
4	0, 1, 2, 3, or 4 real zeros (possible) Or 2 real zeros and 2 complex zeros or 4 complex zeros
…	…

All the zeros of a polynomial satisfy the equation $f(x) = 0$. That is, if k is a zero of a polynomial, then plugging in $x = k$ into the polynomial results in 0. This also means that the polynomial is evenly divisible by the factor $(x - k)$.

All polynomials where n is an odd number will have at least one real zero or root. Complex zeros always come in pairs (specifically, complex conjugate pairs).

GO ON

EXAMPLE

Find the roots of the polynomial: $y = 3t^4 - 48$

Answer:

$y = 3t^4 - 48$	
$3(t^4 - 16) = 0$	Factor the polynomial. Remove the common factor of 3 from each term and make $y = 0$.
$3(t^2 - 4)(t^2 + 4) = 0$ $3(t + 2)(t - 2)(t^2 + 2) = 0$	Factor the difference of squares. $t^2 - 4$ is also a difference of squares.
$t + 2 = 0 \quad t - 2 = 0 \quad t^2 + 2 = 0$ $t = -2 \qquad t = 2 \quad t^2 = -2$ $t = \pm\sqrt{-2} = \pm 2i$ This degree 4 polynomial has four roots, two real roots: **2 or −2**, and two complex roots: **2i or −2i**. The graph will have two x-intercepts at $(-2, 0)$ and $(2, 0)$.	Set each factor equal to zero. Solve each equation.

Rational Functions

Working with Rational Functions

Rational functions are ratios of polynomial functions in the form $f(x) = \frac{g(x)}{h(x)}$. Just like rational numbers, rational functions form a closed system under addition, subtraction, multiplication, and division by a nonzero rational expression. This means adding two rational functions, for example, results in another rational function.

To add or subtract rational expressions, the least common denominator of the factors in the denominator must be found. Then, numerators are added, just like adding rational numbers. To multiply rational expressions, factors can be multiplied straight across, canceling factors that appear in the numerator and denominator. To divide rational functions, use the "invert and multiply" rule.

Rational equations are solved by multiplying through the equation by the least common denominator of factors in the denominator. Just like with radical equations, this process can result in extraneous solutions, so all answers need to be checked by plugging them into the original equation.

EXAMPLES

1) If $f(x) = \frac{2}{3x^2y}$ and $g(x) = \frac{5}{21y}$, find the difference between the functions, $f(x) - g(x)$.

Answer:

$f(x) - g(x) = \frac{2}{3x^2y} - \frac{5}{21y}$	Write the difference.
$= \frac{2}{3x^2y}\left(\frac{7}{7}\right) - \frac{5}{21y}\left(\frac{x^2}{x^2}\right)$ $= \frac{14}{21x^2y} - \frac{5x^2}{21x^2y}$	Figure out the least common denominator. Every factor must be represented to the highest power it appears in either denominator. So, the LCD $= 3(7)x^2y$.
$f(x) - g(x) = \frac{14 - 5x^2}{21x^2y}$	Subtract the numerators the find the answer.

2) If $f(x) = \frac{(x-1)(x+2)^2}{5x^2 + 10x}$ and $g(x) = \frac{x^2 + x - 2}{x + 5}$, find the quotient $\frac{f(x)}{g(x)}$.

Answer:

$\frac{f(x)}{g(x)} = \dfrac{\frac{(x-1)(x+2)^2}{5x^2+10x}}{\frac{x^2+x-2}{x+5}}$ $= \frac{(x-1)(x+2)^2}{5x^2+10x} \times \frac{x+5}{x^2+x-2}$	Write the quotient; then invert and multiply.
$= \frac{(x-1)(x+2)^2}{5x(x+2)} \times \frac{x+5}{(x+2)(x-1)}$	Factor all expressions, and then cancel any factors that appear in both the numerator and the denominator.
$= \frac{x+5}{5x}$	

3) Solve the rational equation $\frac{x}{x+2} + \frac{2}{x^2+5x+6} = \frac{5}{x+3}$.

Answer:

$\frac{x}{x+2} + \frac{2}{x^2+5x+6} = \frac{5}{x+3}$	
$\frac{x}{x+2} + \frac{2}{(x+3)(x+2)} = \frac{5}{x+3}$	Factor any denominators that need factoring.
$x(x+3) + 2 = 5(x+2)$	Multiply through by the LCM of the denominators, which is $(x+2)(x+3)$.
$x^2 + 3x + 2 - 5x - 10 = 0$ $x^2 - 2x - 8 = 0$	Simplify the expression.
$(x-4)(x+2) = 0$	Factor the quadratic.

Plugging $x = -2$ into the original equation results in a 0 in the denominator. So this solution is an extraneous solution and must be thrown out.

Plugging in $x = 4$ gives $\frac{4}{6} + \frac{2}{16 + 20 + 6} = \frac{5}{7}$.

So **$x = 4$** is a solution to the equation.

Graphing Rational Functions

Rations functions are graphed by examining the function to find key features of the graph, including asymptotes, intercepts, and holes.

A **VERTICAL ASYMPTOTE** exists at any value that makes the denominator of a (simplified) rational function equal zero. A vertical asymptote is a vertical line through an *x* value that is not in the domain of the rational function (the function is undefined at this value because division by 0 is not allowed). The function approaches, but never crosses, this line, and the *y* values increase (or decrease) without bound (or "go to infinity") as this *x* value is approached.

To find *x*-intercepts and vertical asymptotes, factor the numerator and denominator of the function. Cancel any terms that appear in the numerator and denominator (if there are any). These values will appear as **HOLES** on the final graph. Since a fraction only equals 0 when its numerator is 0, set the simplified numerator equal to 0 and solve to find the *x*-intercepts. Next, set the denominator equal to 0 and solve to find the vertical asymptotes.

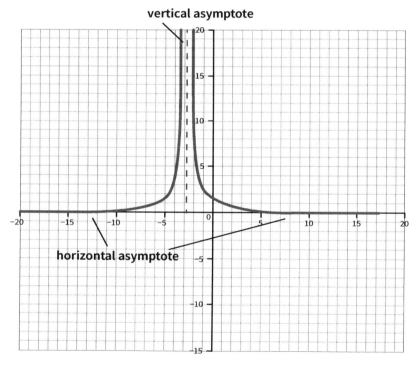

Figure 4.6. Graphing Rational Functions

HORIZONTAL ASYMPTOTES are horizontal lines that describe the "end behavior" of a rational function. In other words, the horizontal asymptote describes what happens to the *y*-values of the function as the *x*-values get very large ($x \rightarrow \infty$) or very small ($x \rightarrow -\infty$). A horizontal asymptote occurs if the degree of the numerator of a rational function is less than or equal to the degree in the denominator. The table summarizes the conditions for horizontal asymptotes:

Table 4.4. Conditions for Horizontal Asymptotes

For polynomials with first terms $\frac{ax^n}{bx^d}$ ...

$n < d$	as $x \to \infty$, $y \to 0$ as $x \to -\infty$, $y \to 0$	The x-axis ($y = 0$) is a horizontal asymptote.
$n = d$	as $x \to \pm\infty$, $y \to \frac{a}{b}$	There is a horizontal asymptote at $y = \frac{a}{b}$.
$n > d$	as $x \to \infty$, $y \to \infty$ or $-\infty$ as $x \to -\infty$, $y \to \infty$ or $-\infty$	There is no horizontal asymptote.

EXAMPLES

1) Graph the function: $f(x) = \frac{3x^2 - 12x}{x^2 - 2x - 3}$.

Answer:

$y = \frac{3x^2 - 12x}{x^2 - 2x - 3}$ $= \frac{3x(x - 4)}{(x - 3)(x + 1)}$	Factor the equation.
$3x(x - 4) = 0$ $x = 0, 4$	Find the roots by setting the numerator equal to zero.
$(x - 3)(x + 1) = 0$ $x = -1, 3$	Find the vertical asymptotes by setting the denominator equal to zero.
The degree of the numerator and denominator are equal, so the asymptote is the ratio of the coefficients: $y = \frac{3}{1} = 3$	Find the horizontal asymptote by looking at the degree of the numerator and the denominator.

Use the roots and asymptotes to graph the function.

GO ON

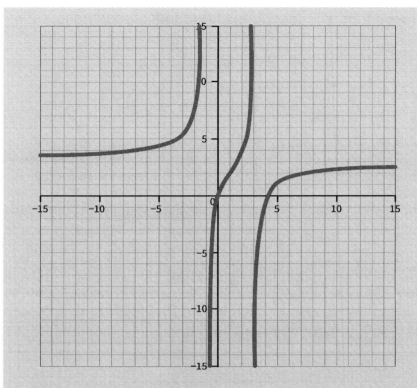

2) Create a function that has an *x*-intercept at (5, 0) and vertical asymptotes at *x* = 1 and *x* = –1.

Answer:

The numerator will have a factor of (*x* – 5) in order to have a zero at *x* = 5. The denominator will need factors of (*x* – 1) and (*x* + 1) in order for the denominator to be 0 when *x* is 1 or –1. Thus, one function that would have these features is

$$y = \frac{(x-5)}{(x+1)(x-1)} = \frac{x-5}{x^2-1}$$

Radical Functions

Radical functions have rational (fractional) exponents, or include the radical symbol. For example, $f(x) = 2(x-5)^{\frac{1}{3}}$ and $g(t) = \sqrt[4]{5-x}$ are radical functions. The domain of even root functions is $0 \le x \le \infty$ and the range is $y \ge 0$. For odd root functions, the domain is all real numbers (because you can take cube roots, etc., of negative numbers). The range is also all real numbers.

To solve equations involving radical functions, first isolate the radical part of the expression. Then "undo" the fractional exponent by raising both sides to the reciprocal of the fractional exponent (for example, undo square roots by squaring both sides). Then solve the equation using inverse operations, as always. All answers should be checked by plugging them back into the original equation, as **EXTRANEOUS SOLUTIONS** result when an equation is raised to powers on both sides. This means there may be some answers that are not actually solutions, and should be eliminated.

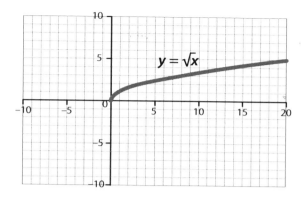

Figure 4.7. Radical Parent Function

EXAMPLES

1) Solve the equation: $\sqrt{2x-5} + 4 = x$

Answer:

$\sqrt{2x-5} + 4 = x$	
$\sqrt{2x-5} = x - 4$	Isolate the $\sqrt{2x-5}$ by subtracting 4.
$2x - 5 = x^2 - 8x + 16$	Square both sides to clear the $\sqrt{\ }$.
$x^2 - 10x + 21 = 0$	Collect all variables to one side.
$(x - 7)(x - 3) = 0$	Factor and solve.
$x = 7$ or $x = 3$	
$\sqrt{2(7)-5} + 4 = 7$	Check solutions by plugging into the original, as squaring both sides can cause extraneous solutions.
$\sqrt{2(3)-5} + 4 = 3$	
$\sqrt{9} + 4 = 7$	True, $x = 7$ is a solution.
$\sqrt{1} + 4 = 3$	False, $x = 3$ is NOT a solution (extraneous solution).
$\boldsymbol{x = 7}$	

2) Solve the equation: $2(x^2 - 7x)^{\frac{2}{3}} = 8$

Answer:

$2(x^2 - 7x)^{\frac{2}{3}} = 8$	
$(x^2 - 7x)^{\frac{2}{3}} = 4$	Divide by 2 to isolate the radical.
$x^2 - 7x = 4^{\frac{3}{2}}$	Raise both sides to the $\frac{3}{2}$ power to clear the $\frac{2}{3}$ exponent.
$x^2 - 7x = 8$	
$x^2 - 7x - 8 = 0$	This is a quadratic, so collect all terms to one side.

$$(x - 8)(x + 1) = 0$$

x = 8 or x = −1

Factor and solve for *x*.

Plugging both solutions into the original equation confirms that both are solutions.

Modeling Relationships

Modeling relationships requires use of one of four of the function types examined above with an appropriate equation for a word problem or scenario.

Table 2.8. Function Types

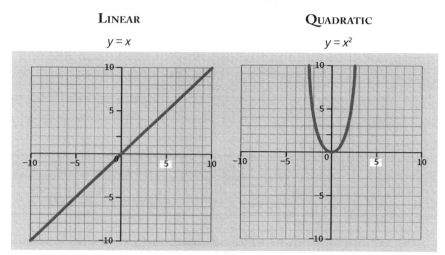

LINEAR

$y = x$

Key words: constant change, slope, equal

QUADRATIC

$y = x^2$

Key words: area, squared, parabola

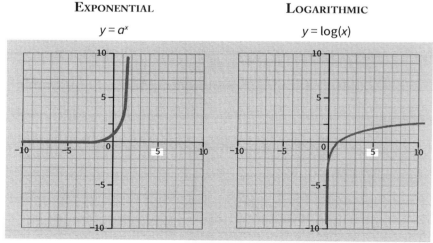

EXPONENTIAL

$y = a^x$

Key words: growth, decay, interest, double, triple, half-life

LOGARITHMIC

$y = \log(x)$

Key words: log-scale, base, log equations

Since exponential functions and log functions are inverses of each other, it will often be the case that exponential or log problems can be solved by either type of equation.

EXAMPLES

1) Consider the following sets of coordinate pairs of a function: $\{(-1, 0.4), (0, 1), (2, 6.25),$ and $(3, 15.625)\}$. What kind of function does this represent?

Answer:

This function is not linear because there is not a constant change in the y value: the slope (rate of change) between $(-1, 0.4)$, and $(0, 1)$ is -0.6, whereas the slope between $(0, 1)$ and $(2, 6.25)$ is 2.625. There is also an x value that is negative, so it cannot be a logarithmic function (the domain of log functions is $x > 0$). Everything has been eliminated except quadratic and exponential. Graphing on the coordiante plane shows what looks like an exponential function.

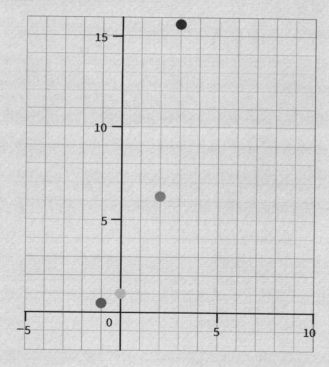

If it is exponential, then its equation is $y = ab^x$, where a is the y-intercept, so $a = 1$ in this case. The b is the growth or decay value. Plug in another point, such as $(2, 6.25)$ to solve for b:

$y = ab^x$

$6.25 = (1)b^2$

$b = \sqrt{6.25} = 2.5$

The equation, then, is $y = 2.5^x$.

Check another point to confirm: Is $0.4 = 2.5^{-1}$? Since $2.5 = \frac{5}{2}$, and $\left(\frac{5}{2}\right)^{-1} = \frac{2}{5} = 0.4$, the equation works. The function is **exponential**.

2) At a recent sporting event, there were 20,000 people in attendance. When it ended, people left the building at a rate of 1,000 people in the first minute, 1,000 more in the second minute, 1,000 in the third minute, and so on. What equation describes the behavior of attendees leaving the event for every minute after the event finished?

Answer:

The dependent variable is the number of attendees leaving the event (y). There is a constant change of 1,000 people per minute. Note that this is an additive pattern in the table: every increase of 1 in time results in a subtraction of the same value (1,000) in y. Because it is a constant rate of change, a linear model is required:

$y = 20,000 - 1,000x$

Here 20,000 is the y-intercept, and the rate of change, $-1,000$, is the slope.

To test this model, confirm that 18,000 attendees were left in the building after two minutes:

$y = 20,000 - 1,000(2) = 18,000$

The model is correct.

five

PRACTICE TEST

Work the problem and choose the most correct answer.

1. To which of the following number sets does 3 not belong?

    A. irrational

    B. rational

    C. whole

    D. integer

    E. real

2. Which inequality is represented by the following graph?

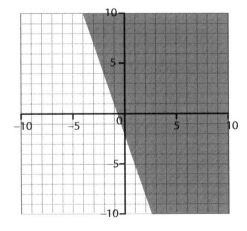

    A. $y \geq -3x - 2$

    B. $y \geq 3x - 2$

    C. $y > -3x - 2$

    D. $y \leq -3x - 2$

    E. $y \geq -3x + 2$

3. If $16^{x+10} = 8^{3x}$, what is the value of x?

    A. 0.5

    B. 2

    C. 4

    D. 5

    E. 8

4. Simplify: $(5 + 2i)(3 + 4i)$

    A. 7

    B. 23

    C. $7 + 26i$

    D. $23 + 26i$

    E. $7 - 26i$

5. The average speed of cars on a highway (s) is inversely proportional to the number of cars on the road (n). If a car drives at 65 mph when there are 250 cars on the road, how fast will a car drive when there are 325 cars on the road?

    A. 50 mph

    B. 55 mph

    C. 60 mph

    D. 85 mph

    E. 87 mph

6. If $j = 4$, what is the value of $2(j - 4)^4 - j + \frac{1}{2}j$?

   A. 0

   B. −2

   C. 2

   D. 4

   E. 32

7. Which of the following is equivalent to $z^3(z + 2)^2 - 4z^3 + 2$?

   A. 2

   B. $z^5 + 4z^4 + 4z^3 + 2$

   C. $z^6 + 4z^3 + 2$

   D. $z^5 + 4z^4 + 2$

   E. $z^5 + 4z^3 + 6$

8. Which of the following is equivalent to $54z^4 + 18z^3 + 3z + 3$?

   A. $18z^4 + 6z^3 + z + 1$

   B. $3z(18z^3 + 6z^2 + 1)$

   C. $3(18z^4 + 6z^3 + z + 1)$

   D. $72z^7 + 3z$

   E. $54(z^4 + 18z^3 + 3z + 3)$

9. Which of the following is the y-intercept of the given equation?

   $7y - 42x + 7 = 0$

   A. $(0, \frac{1}{6})$

   B. $(6, 0)$

   C. $(0, -1)$

   D. $(-1, 0)$

   E. $(0, 7)$

10. Simplify: $(1.2 \times 10^{-3})(1.13 \times 10^{-4})$

    A. 1.356×10^{-12}

    B. 1.356×10^{-7}

    C. 1.356×10^{-1}

    D. 1.356×10

    E. 1.356×10^{12}

11. Which of the following represents a linear equation?

    A. $\sqrt[3]{y} = x$

    B. $\sqrt[3]{x} = y$

    C. $\sqrt[3]{y} = x^2$

    D. $y = \sqrt[6]{x^3}$

    E. $y = \sqrt[3]{x^3}$

12. Which of the following is a solution of the given equation?

    $4(m + 4)^2 - 4m^2 + 20 = 276$

    A. 3

    B. 4

    C. 6

    D. 12

    E. 24

13. If the length of a rectangle is increased by 40% and its width is decreased by 40%, what is the effect on the rectangle's area?

    A. The area is the same.

    B. It increases by 16%.

    C. It increases by 20%.

    D. It decreases by 16%.

    E. It decreases by 20%.

14. Which of the following numbers is NOT rational?

    I. π

    II. $\frac{13}{5}$

    III. $7.\overline{45}$

    A. I only

    B. II only

    C. I and III only

    D. II and III only

    E. I, II, and III

15. What is the x-intercept of the given equation?

$10x + 10y = 10$

A. $(1, 0)$

B. $(0, 1)$

C. $(0, 0)$

D. $(1, 1)$

E. $(10, 10)$

16. What is the value of z in the following system?

$z - 2x = 14$

$2z - 6x = 18$

A. -7

B. -2

C. 3

D. 5

E. 24

17. Simplify: $-(3^2) + (5 - 7)^2 - 3(4 - 8)$

A. -25

B. -17

C. -1

D. 7

E. 25

18. Which of the following is a solution to the inequality $2x + y \leq -10$?

A. $(0, 0)$

B. $(10, 2)$

C. $(10, 10)$

D. $(-10, -10)$

E. $(0, 10)$

19. Find $(f - g)(x)$ if $f(x) = x^2 + 16x$ and $g(x) = 5x^2 + 4x + 25$.

A. $-4x^2 + 12x - 25$

B. $-4x^2 - 12x - 25$

C. $-4x^2 - 20x + 25$

D. $4x^2 - 20x - 25$

E. $4x^2 + 12x - 25$

20. If the water in a reservoir decreases every day by 4%, by how much will the water decrease over a 7-day week?

A. 24.9%

B. 28.0%

C. 32.4%

D. 96.0%

E. 131.6%

21. 50 shares of a financial stock and 10 shares of an auto stock are valued at $1,300. If 10 shares of the financial stock and 10 shares of the auto stock are valued at $500, what is the value of 50 shares of the auto stock?

A. $30

B. $20

C. $1,300

D. $1,500

E. $1,800

22. Find $f(x) = (j \circ t)(x)$ if $j(x) = \frac{1}{3}x - 2$ and $t(x) = \frac{1}{2}x - 3$.

A. $f(x) = \frac{1}{6}x^2 + 6$

B. $f(x) = \frac{1}{6}x^2 - 5x + 6$

C. $f(x) = \frac{1}{6}x - 4$

D. $f(x) = \frac{1}{6}x - 3$

E. $f(x) = \frac{1}{6}x - 1$

23. In a class of 20 students, how many conversations must be had so that every student talks to every other student in the class?

A. 40

B. 190

C. 380

D. 760

E. 6840

24. What are the roots of the function $f(x) = 4x^2 - 6x + 7$?

A. $\left\{ \dfrac{3+i\sqrt{19}}{4}, \dfrac{3-i\sqrt{19}}{4} \right\}$

B. $\{0, 2\}$

C. $\left\{ \dfrac{6+\sqrt{-76}}{4}, \dfrac{6-\sqrt{76}}{4} \right\}$

D. $\left\{ \dfrac{3+i\sqrt{5}}{4}, \dfrac{3-i\sqrt{5}}{4} \right\}$

E. $\left\{ \dfrac{3+\sqrt{19}}{4}, \dfrac{3-\sqrt{19}}{4} \right\}$

25. Which of the following is the solution set to the given inequality?

$2x + 4 \geq 5(x - 4) - 3(x - 4)$

A. $(-\infty, \infty)$

B. $(-\infty, 6.5]$

C. $[6.5, -\infty)$

D. $(-\infty, 6.5) \cup (6.5, \infty)$

E. $\varnothing$

26. The line $f(x)$ is shown on the graph below. If $g(x) = f(x - 2) + 3$, which of the following points lies on $g(x)$?

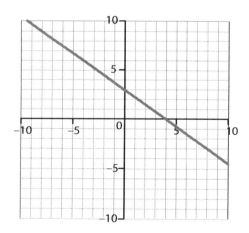

A. $(1, 2)$

B. $(2, 3)$

C. $(4, 0)$

D. $(6, 3)$

E. $(7, 2)$

27. What are the real zero(s) of the following polynomial?

$2n^2 + 2n - 12 = 0$

A. $\{-3, 2\}$

B. $\{2\}$

C. $\{2, 0\}$

D. $\{2, 4\}$

E. There are no real zeros of n.

28. What are the roots of the equation $y = 16x^3 - 48x^2$?

A. $\left\{ \dfrac{3+i\sqrt{5}}{2}, \dfrac{3-i\sqrt{5}}{2} \right\}$

B. $\{0, 3, -3\}$

C. $\{0, 3i, -3i\}$

D. $\{0, 3\}$

E. $\{0\}$

29. Which of the following defines y as a function of x?

I. $y^2 + x = 3$

II.

x	y
0	4
1	5
2	8
3	13
4	20

III.

$y = \sin(\theta)$

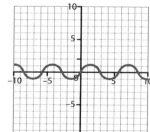

A. none

B. II only

C. I and II only

D. II and III only

E. I, II, III only

30. Simplify: $\frac{3+\sqrt{3}}{4-\sqrt{3}}$

A. $\frac{13}{15}$

B. $-\frac{1}{4}$

C. $\frac{15+7\sqrt{3}}{13}$

D. $\frac{15}{19}$

E. $\frac{15+7\sqrt{3}}{19}$

31. What is the axis of symmetry for the given parabola?

$y = -2(x+3)^2 + 5$

A. $y = 3$

B. $x = -3$

C. $y = -3$

D. $x = 3$

E. $x = 5$

32. Find the 12th term of the following sequence.

$-57, -40, -23, -6...$

A. 57

B. 79

C. 113

D. 130

E. 147

33. The number of individuals, *N*, in a certain population of deer is expected to increase every year by 5 percent. If the current population is 14,300 individuals, which of the following best describes the size of the population in *t* years?

A. $N(t) = 14,300(0.05)^t$

B. $N(t) = 14,300(1.05)^t$

C. $N(t) = 14,300^{1.05t}$

D. $N(t) = 14,300^{0.05t}$

E. $N(t) = 14,300^{0.5t}$

34. What is the domain of the inequality $\left|\frac{x}{8}\right| \geq 1$?

A. $(-\infty, \infty)$

B. $[8, \infty)$

C. $(-\infty, -8]$

D. $(-\infty, -8] \cup [8, \infty)$

E. $\varnothing$

35. Which of the following are the vertical asymptotes of the given function?

$f(x) = \frac{x^3 - 16x}{-4x^2 + 4x + 24}$

A. $x = -4$ and $x = 4$

B. $x = -3$ and $x = 2$

C. $x = -2$ and $x = 3$

D. $x = 0$ and $x = 4$

E. $x = 0$ and $x = 2$

36. What is the solution set for the inequality $2x^2 - 4x - 6 < 0$?

A. $(-1, 3)$

B. $(-\infty, \infty)$

C. $\varnothing$

D. $(-\infty, -1) \cup (3, \infty)$

E. $(-1, \infty)$

37. What is the greatest number of complex roots a 17th degree polynomial can have?

A. 8

B. 15

C. 16

D. $16i$

E. 17

38. $(3x + 2)^2 =$

A. $9x^2 + 4$

B. $9x^2 + 36$

C. $9x^2 + 6x + 4$

D. $9x^2 + 10x + 4$

E. $9x^2 + 12x + 4$

39. The population of a city in 2008 was 1.25 million people. If the population is decreasing by 5% annually, in what year will the population reach 1 million?

A. 2011

B. 2012

C. 2013

D. 2014

E. 2015

40. Valerie receives a base salary of $740 a week for working 40 hours. For every extra hour she works, she is paid at a rate of $27.75 per hour. If Valerie works t hours in a week, which of the following equations represents the amount of money, A, she will receive?

A. $A = 740 + 27.75(t - 40)$

B. $A = 740 + 27.75(40 - t)$

C. $A = 740 - 27.75(40 - t)$

D. $A = 27.75t - 740$

E. $A = 27.75t + 740$

41. Which expression is equivalent to $\log_6 \left(\frac{36}{x} \right)$?

A. $2 - x$

B. $6 - \log x$

C. $2 - \log_6 x$

D. $\log_6 x - 2$

E. $(\log_6 x)^2$

42. Which of the following is an equation of the line that passes through the points $(4, -3)$ and $(-2, 9)$ in the xy-plane?

A. $y = -2x + 5$

B. $y = -\frac{1}{2}x - 1$

C. $y = \frac{1}{2}x - 5$

D. $y = 2x - 11$

E. $y = 4x + 1$

43. Simplify: $\frac{3}{2-i}$

A. $2 + i$

B. $6 + 3i$

C. $\frac{2+i}{5}$

D. $\frac{6+3i}{5}$

E. $\frac{3}{2} - \frac{3}{i}$

44. What is the value of z in the following equation?

$\log_7(-2z) = 0$

A. $-\frac{1}{2}$

B. 0

C. $\frac{1}{2}$

D. 1

E. $\frac{7}{2}$

45. Which value is equivalent to $5^2 \times (-5)^{-2} - (2 + 3)^{-1}$?

A. 0

B. $\frac{4}{5}$

C. 1

D. $\frac{5}{4}$

E. 2

46. What are the zeros of $\left(\frac{g}{h} \right)(k)$ if $g(k) = -3k^2 - k$ and $h(k) = -2k - 4$?

A. $\left\{ 0, \frac{1}{3} \right\}$

B. $\{-2\}$

C. $\{0\}$

D. $\left\{ -2, 0, \frac{1}{3} \right\}$

E. $\{-2, 0\}$

47. What are the values of a for which $\frac{1}{(a-1)} = \frac{1}{6} + \frac{1}{a}$?

A. $a = 3$ only

B. $a = -2$ only

C. $a = -2$ and $x = 3$

D. $a = 1$ and $a = 3$

E. There are no real solutions.

48. If $\dfrac{4x-5}{3} = \dfrac{\frac{1}{2}(2x-6)}{5}$, what is the value of x?

A. $-\dfrac{2}{7}$

B. $-\dfrac{4}{17}$

C. $\dfrac{16}{17}$

D. 1

E. $\dfrac{8}{7}$

49. The number of chairs in the front row of a movie theater is 14. Each subsequent row contains 2 more seats than the row in front of it. If the theater has 25 rows, what is the total number of seats in the theater?

A. 336

B. 350

C. 888

D. 950

E. 1014

50. If $f(x) = 2x^2 + 6$, what is its inverse, $f(x)^{-1}$?

A. $f(x)^{-1} = \sqrt{\dfrac{x-6}{2}}$

B. $f(x)^{-1} = \sqrt{\dfrac{x+6}{2}}$

C. $f(x)^{-1} = 2\sqrt{x-6}$

D. $f(x)^{-1} = \sqrt{\dfrac{x+6}{2}}$

E. $f(x)^{-1} = \sqrt{\dfrac{x-6}{2}}$

51. The inequality $6 > x^2 - x$ is true for which of the following values of x?

I. $x < -2$

II. $-2 < x < -3$

III. $x > 3$

A. I only

B. II only

C. III only

D. I and III only

E. I, II, and III

52. In the xy-plane, the line given by which of the following equations is parallel to the line $3x + 2y = 10$?

A. $y = -3x + 2$

B. $y = -\dfrac{3}{2}x - 10$

C. $y = \dfrac{1}{3}x + 5$

D. $y = \dfrac{2}{3}x - 10$

E. $y = 5x + 2$

53. Simplify: $\dfrac{12!\,2!}{10!\,3!}$

A. 22

B. 44

C. 66

D. 88

E. 121

54. What is the value of $f(2)$ for the function $(x) = 0.5^x + \log_4 x$?

A. 0.25

B. 0.5

C. 0.75

D. 3

E. 4.5

55. The line of best fit is calculated for a data set that tracks the number of miles that passenger cars traveled annually in the US from 1960 to 2010. In the model, $x = 0$ represents the year 1960, and y is the number of miles traveled in billions. If the line of best fit is $y = 0.0293x + 0.563$, approximately how many additional miles were traveled for every 5 years that passed?

A. 0.0293 billion

B. 0.1465 billion

C. 0.5630 billion

D. 0.7100 billion

E. 2.9615 billion

56. The table below shows values of the function $g(x)$. If g is an even function, what are the missing values?

x	g(x)
−4	6
−2	−3
0	0
2	
4	

57. If $y = 2x^2 + 12x - 3$ is written if the form $y = a(x - h)^2 + k$, what is the value of k?

A. −2

B. −3

C. −15

D. −18

E. −21

58. When $\frac{5 + 2i}{3 - i}$ is expressed in the form $a + bi$, what is the value of b?

59. In the following graph of $f(x) = y$, for how many values of x does $|f(x)| = 1$?

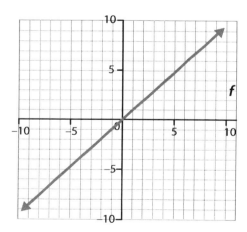

A. 0

B. 1

C. 2

D. 4

E. ∞

60. Which of the following represents the range of the function $(x) = |x - a| + b$?

A. $(-\infty, \infty)$

B. $(-\infty, a]$

C. $[a, \infty)$

D. $(-\infty, b]$

E. $[b, \infty)$

ANSWER KEY

1. **A)**

   The number 3 is not irrational because it can be written as the fraction $\frac{3}{1}$.

2.

   Eliminate answer choices that don't match the graph.

   A. Correct.

   B. The graph has a negative slope while this inequality has a positive slope.

   C. The line on the graph is solid, so the inequality should include the "or equal to" symbol.

   D. The shading is above the line, meaning the inequality should be "y is greater than."

   E. The y-intercept is −2, not 2.

3. **E)**

   Rewrite the bases so they are the same, then set the exponents equal and solve.

   $16^{x+10} = 8^{3x}$

   $(2^4)^{x+10} = (2^3)^{3x}$

   $2^{4x+40} = 2^{9x}$

   $4x + 40 = 9x$

   $\boldsymbol{x = 8}$

4. **C)**

   FOIL and combine like terms.

   $(5 + 2i)(3 + 4i)$

   $= 15 + 6i + 20i + 8i^2$

   $= 15 + 6i + 20i + (8)(-1)$

   $= 15 + 6i + 20i - 8$

   $\boldsymbol{= 7 + 26i}$

5. **A)**

   Use the formula for inversely proportional relationships to find k and then solve for s.

   $sn = k$

   $(65)(250) = k$

   $k = 16{,}250$

   $s(325) = 16{,}250$

   $s = \boldsymbol{50}$

6. **B)**

   Plug 4 in for j and simplify.

   $2(j - 4)^4 - j + \frac{1}{2}j$

   $2(4 - 4)^4 - 4 + \frac{1}{2}(4) = \boldsymbol{-2}$

7. **D)**

   Simplify using PEMDAS.

   $z^3(z + 2)^2 - 4z^3 + 2$

   $z^3(z^2 + 4z + 4) - 4z^3 + 2$

   $z^5 + 4z^4 + 4z^3 - 4z^3 + 2$

   $\boldsymbol{z^5 + 4z^4 + 2}$

8. **C)**

Factor the expression using the greatest common factor of 3.

$54z^4 + 18z^3 + 3z + 3 =$

$\mathbf{3(18z^4 + 6z^3 + z + 1)}$

9. **C)**

Plug 0 in for x and solve for y.

$7y - 42x + 7 = 0$

$7y - 42(0) + 7 = 0$

$y = -1$

The y-intercept is at **(0, −1)**.

10. **B)**

Multiply the digits and add the exponents.

$(1.2 \times 10^{-3})(1.13 \times 10^{-4})$

$1.2 \times 1.13 = 1.356$

$-3 + (-4) = -7$

$\mathbf{1.356 \times 10^{-7}}$

11. **E)**

Solve each equation for y and find the equation with a power of 1.

$\sqrt[3]{y} = x \rightarrow y = x^3$

$\sqrt[3]{x} = y \rightarrow y = \sqrt[3]{x}$

$\sqrt[3]{y} = x^2 \rightarrow y = x^6$

$y = \sqrt[6]{x^3} \rightarrow y = x^{1/2}$

$y = \sqrt[3]{x^3} \rightarrow \mathbf{y = x}$

12. **C)**

Plug each value into the equation.

$4(3 + 4)^2 - 4(3)^2 + 20 = 180 \neq 276$

$4(4 + 4)^2 - 4(3)^2 + 20 = 240 \neq 276$

$4(6 + 4)^2 - 4(6)^2 + 20 = \mathbf{276}$

$4(12 + 4)^2 - 4(12)^2 + 20 = 468 \neq 276$

$4(24 + 4)^2 - 4(24)^2 + 20 = 852 \neq 276$

13. **D)**

Use the formula for the area of a rectangle to find the increase in its size.

$A = lw$

$A = (1.4l)(0.6w)$

$A = 0.84lw$

The new area will be 84% of the original area, a decrease of **16%**.

14. **A)**

I. π is an irrational number because it cannot be simplified as a fraction.

II. $\frac{13}{5}$ is a fraction, so it is rational.

III. $7.\overline{45}$ can be written as the fraction $\frac{82}{11}$, so it is rational.

15. **A)**

Plug 0 in for y and solve for x.

$10x + 10y = 10$

$10x + 10(0) = 10$

$x = 1$

The x-intercept is at **(1, 0)**.

16. **E)**

Solve the system using substitution.

$z - 2x = 14 \rightarrow z = 2x + 14$

$2z - 6x = 18$

$2(2x + 14) - 6x = 18$

$4x + 28 - 6x = 18$

$-2x = -10$

$x = 5$

$z - 2(5) = 14$

$\mathbf{z = 24}$

17. **D)**

Simplify using PEMDAS.

$-(3^2) + (5 - 7)^2 - 3(4 - 8)$

$= -(3^2) + (-2)^2 - 3(-4)$

$= -9 + 4 - 3(-4)$

$= -9 + 4 + 12 = \mathbf{7}$

18. **D)**

Plug in each set of values and determine if the inequality is true.

$2(0) + 0 \leq -10$ FALSE

$2(10) + 2 \leq -10$ FALSE

$2(10) + 10 \leq -10$ FALSE

$2(-10) + (-10) \leq -10$ TRUE

$2(0) + 10 \leq -10$ FALSE

19. **A)**

Subtract $g(x)$ from $f(x)$.

$x^2 + 16x - (5x^2 + 4x + 25) = x^2 + 16x - 5x^2$

$- 4x - 25 = \mathbf{-4x^2 + 12x - 25}$

88 Accepted, Inc. | CLEP College Algebra Study Guide 2017

20. **A)**

Use the exponential decay function. The value $\frac{y}{a}$ represents the percent of the water remaining.

$$y = a(1 - r)^t$$
$$y = (1 - 0.04)^7$$
$$y = (0.96)^7 = 0.751$$

After 7 days, the new amount of water is 0.751, or 75.1% of the original amount. It has decreased by $100 - 75.1 = $ **24.9%**.

21. **D)**

Set up a system of equations and solve using elimination.

$f = $ the cost of a financial stock
$a = $ the cost of an auto stock

$$50f + 10a = 1300$$
$$10f + 10a = 500$$

$$50f + 10a = 1300$$
$$+ \, -50f - 50a = -2500$$
$$-40a = -1{,}200$$
$$a = 30$$
$$50(30) = \textbf{1{,}500}$$

22. **D)**

To find the compound function, substitute $t(x)$ for x in $j(x)$.

$$(j \circ t)(x) = \tfrac{1}{3}\left(\tfrac{1}{2}x - 3\right) - 2 = \tfrac{1}{6}x - 3$$

23. **B)**

Use the combination formula to find the number of ways to choose 2 people out of a group of 20.

$$C(20, 2) = \frac{20!}{2! \, 18!} = \textbf{190}$$

24. **A)**

Use the quadratic formula.

$$f(x) = 4x^2 - 6x + 7$$
$$x = \frac{-(-6) \pm \sqrt{(-6)^2 - 4(4)(7)}}{2(4)}$$
$$x = \frac{3 \pm i\sqrt{19}}{4}$$

25. **A)**

Simplify the inequality.

$$2x + 4 \ge 5x - 20 - 3x + 12$$
$$2x + 4 \ge 2x - 8$$

$$4 \ge -8$$

Since the inequality is always true, the solution is all real numbers, $(-\infty, \infty)$.

26. **C)**

The function $g(x) = f(x - 2) + 3$ is a translation of $\langle 2, 3 \rangle$ from $f(x)$. Test each possible point by undoing the transformation and checking if the point lies on $f(x)$.

$(1, 2) \rightarrow (-1, -1)$: This point is not on $f(x)$.

$(2, 3) \rightarrow (0, 0)$: This point is not on $f(x)$.

$(4, 0) \rightarrow (2, -3)$: This point is not on $f(x)$.

$(6, 3) \rightarrow (4, 0)$: **This point is on $f(x)$.**

$(7, 2) \rightarrow (5, -1)$: This point is not on $f(x)$.

27. **A)**

Factor the trinomial and set each factor equal to 0.

$$2n^2 + 2n - 12 = 0$$
$$2(n^2 + n - 6) = 0$$
$$2(n + 3)(n - 2) = 0$$
$$\textbf{\textit{n} = -3 and \textit{n} = 2}$$

28. **D)**

Factor the equation and set each factor equal to 0.

$$y = 16x^3 - 48x^2$$
$$16x^2(x - 3) = 0$$
$$\textbf{\textit{x} = 0 and \textit{x} = 3}$$

29. **C)**

Only I and II define y as a function of x.

I. This is not a function: the equation represents a horizontal parabola, which fails the vertical line test.

II. This is a function: each x-value corresponds to only one y-value.

III. This is a function: the graph passes the vertical line test.

30. **C)**

Multiply by the complex conjugate and simplify.

$$\frac{3 + \sqrt{3}}{4 - \sqrt{3}}\left(\frac{4 + \sqrt{3}}{4 + \sqrt{3}}\right)$$
$$= \frac{12 + 4\sqrt{3} + 3\sqrt{3} + 3}{16 - 4\sqrt{3} + 4\sqrt{3} - 3} = \frac{\textbf{15} + \textbf{7}\sqrt{\textbf{3}}}{\textbf{13}}$$

31. **B)**

The axis of symmetry will be a vertical line that runs through the vertex, which is the point $(-3, 5)$. The line of symmetry is $x = -3$.

32. **D)**

Use the equation to find the nth term of an arithmetic sequence.

$a_1 = -57$

$d = -40 - (-57) = 17$

$n = 12$

$a_n = a_1 + d(n - 1)$

$a_{12} = -57 + 17(12 - 1)$

$\boldsymbol{a_{12} = 130}$

33. **B)**

The population is growing exponentially, so plug the values into the equation for exponential growth.

$A(t) = a(1 + r)^t$

$N(t) = 14,300(1 + 0.05)^t$

$\boldsymbol{N(t) = 14,300(1.05)^t}$

34. **D)**

Split the absolute value inequality into two inequalities and simplify. Switch the inequality when making one side negative.

$\frac{x}{8} \geq 1$

$x \geq 8$

$-\frac{x}{8} \geq 1$

$\frac{x}{8} \leq -1$

$x \leq -8$

$x \leq -8$ or $x \geq 8 \rightarrow \boldsymbol{(-\infty, -8] \cup [8, \infty)}$

35. **C)**

Make sure there are no factors that cancel, and then set the denominator equal to 0.

$\frac{x^3 - 16x}{-4x^2 + 4x + 24} = \frac{x(x^2 - 16)}{-4(x^2 - x - 6)}$

$= \frac{x(x + 4)(x - 4)}{-4(x - 3)(x + 2)}$

The graph has no holes.

$-4(x - 3)(x + 2) = 0$

$\boldsymbol{x = 3}$ and $\boldsymbol{x = -2}$

36. **A)**

Use the zeros of the function to find the intervals where it is less than 0.

$2x^2 - 4x - 6 = 0$

$(2x - 6)(x + 1) = 0$

$x = 3$ and $x = -1$

$(-\infty, -1) \rightarrow 2x^2 - 4x - 6 > 0$

$(-1, 3) \rightarrow 2x^2 - 4x - 6 < 0$

$(3, \infty) \rightarrow 2x^2 - 4x - 6 > 0$

The function is less than 0 on the interval $\boldsymbol{(-1, 3)}$.

37. **C)**

Complex solutions always come in pairs. Therefore, the number of possible complex solutions is the greatest *even* number equal to or less than the power of the polynomial. A 17th degree polynomial can have at most **16** complex roots.

38. **E)**

Use FOIL to solve.

$(3x + 2)(3x + 2) = 9x^2 + 6x + 6x + 4 = \boldsymbol{9x^2 + 12x + 4}$

39. **C)**

Use the equation for exponential decay to find the year the population reached 1 million.

$y = a(1 - r)^t$

$y = 1250000(1 - 0.05)^t$

$1,000,000 = 1250000(1 - 0.05)^t$

$0.8 = 0.95^t$

$\log_{0.8} 0.8 = \log_{0.8} 0.95^t$

$1 = t \times \frac{\log 0.95}{\log .8}$

$t = 4.35$

The population will reach 1 million in 2013.

40. **A)**

Valerie will receive her base pay plus 27.75 for every hour she worked in addition to her 40 hours.

$A = $ base pay $+ 27.75 \times$ extra hours

$\boldsymbol{A = 740 + 27.75(t - 40)}$

41. **C)**

Expand the original expression using the properties of logarithms.

$\log_6\left(\frac{36}{x}\right) = \log_6(36) - \log_6(x) =$

$2 - \log_6 x$

42. **A)**

Use the points to find the slope.

$m = \frac{y_2 - y_1}{x_2 - x_1} = \frac{-3 - 9}{4 - (-2)} = -2$

Use the point-slope equation to find the equation of the line.

$(y - y_1) = m(x - x\_1)$

$y - (-3) = -2(x - 4)$

$y = -2x + 5$

43. **D)**

Multiply by the complex conjugate and simplify.

$\frac{3}{2-i}$

Multiply: $\left(\frac{3}{2-i}\right)\left(\frac{2+i}{2+i}\right)$

$\frac{3(2+i)}{4 - 2i + 2i - i^2}$

$= \frac{3(2+i)}{4 - (-1)}$

$= \frac{(6 + 3i)}{5}$

44. **A)**

Rewrite the equation in exponential form and solve.

$\log_7(-2z) = 0$

$7^0 = -2z$

$1 = -2z$

$z = -\frac{1}{2}$

45. **B)**

Simplify using PEMDAS.

$5^2 \times (-5)^{-2} - 5^{-1}$

$= 25 \times \frac{1}{25} - \frac{1}{5}$

$= 1 - \frac{1}{5}$

$= \frac{4}{5}$

46. **A)**

Set the numerator of the resulting rational function equal to 0 to find the zeros.

$\left(\frac{g}{h}\right)(k) = \frac{(-3k^2 - k)}{(-2k - 4)}$

$0 = 3k^2 - k$

$0 = k(3k - 1)$

$k = 0, \frac{1}{3}$

47. **C)**

Multiply by the LCD and solve for a.

$6a(a - 1)\left[\frac{1}{a-1} = \frac{1}{6} + \frac{1}{a}\right]$

$6a = a(a - 1) + 6(a - 1)$

$6a = (a + 6)(a - 1)$

$0 = a^2 - a - 6$

$0 = (x + 2)(x - 3)$

$x = -2$ and $x = 3$

48. **C)**

Cross multiply and solve for x.

$\frac{4x - 5}{3} = \frac{\frac{1}{2}(2x - 6)}{5}$

$5(4x - 5) = \frac{3}{2}(2x - 6)$

$20x - 25 = 3x - 9$

$17x = 16$

$x = \frac{16}{17}$

49. **D)**

Use the formula for an arithmetic sum.

$S_n = \frac{n}{2}(2a_1 + (n - 1)d)$

$= \frac{25}{2}(2(14) + (25 - 1)2) = \mathbf{950}$

50. **A)**

Swap x and y in the equation, then solve for y.

$f(x) = 2x^2 + 6$

$y = 2x^2 + 6$

$x = 2y^2 + 6$

$y = \sqrt{\frac{x - 6}{2}}$

51. **B)**

Move the terms to the same side and factor. Use the zeros to find the intervals where the inequality is true.

$6 > x^2 - x$

$0 > x^2 - x - 6$

$0 > (x + 2)(x - 3)$

For $x < -2$:

$0 \not> (x + 2)(x - 3)$

For $-2 < x < -3$:

$0 > (x + 2)(x - 3)$

For $x > 3$:

$0 \not> (x + 2)(x - 3)$

52. B)

Find the slope of the given line. Any parallel lines will have the same slope.

$3x + 2y = 10$

$2y = -3x + 10$

$y = -\frac{3}{2}x + 5$

53. B)

Cancel terms that appear on the top and bottom, and then mulitply.

$\frac{12!\,2!}{10!\,3!}$

$= \frac{12 \times 11 \times 10! \times 2 \times 1}{10! \times 3 \times 2 \times 1}$

$= \frac{132}{3} = 44$

54. C)

Substitute $x = 2$ in the equation and simplify.

$f(x) = 0.5^x + \log_4{}^x$

$f(2) = 0.5^2 + \log_4 2$

$f(2) = 0.25 + 0.5 = 0.75$

55. B)

The slope 0.0293 gives the increase in passenger car miles (in billions) for each year that passes. Muliply this value by 5 to find the increase that occurs over 5 years: $5(0.0293) = 0.1465$ **billion miles**.

56.

If the function is even, it is symmetric about the y-axis, meaning $f(x) = f(-x)$.

x	$g(x)$
−4	6
−2	−3
0	0
2	−3
4	6

57. E)

Complete the square to put the quadratic equation in vertex form.

$y = 2x^2 + 12x - 3$

$y = 2(x^2 + 6x + \underline{\hspace{1cm}}) - 3 + \underline{\hspace{1cm}}$

$y = 2(x^2 + 6x + 9) - 3 - 18$

$y = 2(x + 3)2 - 21$

58.

Multiply the numerator and denominator by the conjugate of the denominator, and put the equation into $a + bi$ form.

$\left(\frac{5 + 2i}{3 - i}\right) \times \left(\frac{3 + i}{3 + i}\right)$

$\frac{15 + 5i + 6i - 2i^2}{9 - 3i + 3i - i^2}$

$\frac{13 + 11i}{10} = \frac{13}{10} + \frac{11}{10}i$ **or 1.1**

59. C)

The absolute value of $f(x)$ equals 1 twice: once in quadrant I and once in quadrant III.

60. E)

The range of the absolute value parent function is $[0, \infty)$, Function $f(x)$ has been shifted up b units, so the new range is $[b, \infty)$.

Made in the USA
San Bernardino, CA
02 July 2017